Inside Mrs. B's Classroom

Courage, Hope, and Learning on Chicago's South Side

Inside Mrs. B's Classroom

Courage, Hope, and Learning on Chicago's South Side

Leslie Baldacci

McGraw-Hill
New York   Chicago   San Francisco   Lisbon
London   Madrid   Mexico City   Milan   New Delhi
San Juan   Seoul   Singapore   Sydney   Toronto

4 5 6 7 8 9 0   FGR/FGR   0 9 8 7 6 5

ISBN 0-07-141735-4

Printed and bound by Quebecor/Fairfield.

McGraw-Hill books are available at special quantity discounts to use as premiums and sales promotions, or for use in corporate training programs. For more information, please write to the Director of Special Sales, Professional Publishing, McGraw-Hill, Two Penn Plaza, New York, NY 10121-2298. Or contact your local bookstore.

 This book is printed on recycled, acid-free paper containing a minimum of 50% recycled, de-inked fiber.

Library of Congress Cataloging-in-Publication Data

Baldacci, Leslie.
    Inside Mrs. B's classroom : courage, hope, and learning on Chicago's South Side / Leslie Baldacci.
        p.   cm.
    ISBN 0-07-141735-4 (hardcover : alk. paper)
    1. Baldacci, Leslie.   2. Teachers—Illinois—Chicago—Biography.   3. Education, Urban—Illinois—Chicago.   4. Children with social disabilities—Education (Middle school)—Illinois—Chicago.   I. Title.
LA2317.B26   2003
373.236'09773'11—dc22

                                                                        2003019331

For Donna

To the Reader

This book is a factual account of my two years as a rookie teacher in a public school on the South Side of Chicago. The names of some adults and all of the children have been altered or left out altogether to protect their privacy. Some characters were combined and some details jumbled to further disguise the identities of the children.

Contents

Acknowledgments

Thanks to the teachers for their example, especially the Gernands, George and Rita, Pat and Jay, Mary and Bernadette, Ed Baldacci, Florence Baldacci, Glenn and Sue Pawlak, Fred Dobrinski, Donna-maria Gamble Baker, Judy Gouwens, Alonza Everage, Rochelle Lee, Barbara Dress, James Marshall, Minnie Tyrie, Ramona Schwartz, Michelle Navarre, Frank Tobin, Pam Sanders, Fred Chesek, Maria Hernandez-Van Nest and Bill Crannell.

Thanks to Richard Roeper, Mark Jacob, Cristi Kempf, John O'Malley, Ellen Skerrett, Mary Mitchell, Lorrie Lynch, Jeff Bailey, Jeanne Wright, Michelle Bearden, William McGrath and the "sibs," Jeff, Beth and David for counsel and encouragement.

Thanks to Ken Rolling and Marianne Philbin and the Chicago Annenberg Challenge for starting the ball rolling.

Thanks to the book ladies: Janet Rosen, Barbara Gilson and Betsy Lancefield Lane.

Thanks to Artie, Natalie and Mia for your faith and courage on the adventure that changed all of our lives.

Thanks to Joan Dameron Crisler for believing in me. Thanks to my students, in my heart always.

Chapter 1

The Mad Crapper

It was the first time I'd been down to "The Dungeon." The others were already there. A haze of cigarette smoke layered the ancient boiler room, lending a comic twist to the yellow "Warning! Asbestos!" signs on every wall.

Sculptured nails tapped an ash into an overflowing ashtray that sat atop a broken, gutted desk, its drawers long gone. Chairs in various states of disrepair and other junk cluttered the perimeter. Pipes twisted this way and that on the ceilings and walls, taped and painted over in a pitiful attempt to contain the deadly asbestos that had insulated the pipes for decades. I looked around the floor for piles of white dust that were the telltale sign of danger. What was I going to do if I saw some? Call the health department?

"The Dungeon" was the smokers' secret hangout. Board of education rules prohibited teachers from smoking on school property. But the stress of the job was high. Sometimes the only relief was to cadge a smoke on the sly during school hours before facing the cruel crowd again.

Donna opened the meeting.

"Basically, we're gonna have to scare the living shit out of these little fuckers," she declared, blowing out a cloud of smoke. "If they don't shape up, it's no more departmental. We'll be self-contained, and every one of us will have to teach all subjects to the same kids all day."

We all groaned in agony at the thought of being held hostage by our respective classes. This was seventh and eighth grade in a poverty-level, urban school on the South Side of Chicago. Our classes were bursting at the seams with thirty-five, thirty-six and thirty-seven kids apiece.

Tough kids, many of them raising themselves in tough circumstances. There was barely room to walk around the classrooms for all the desks. When the kids were in the room, there was no room left. The noise and heat levels were like a steel mill. The only thing worse than teaching one subject to all four classes every day would be teaching all subjects to the same class all day long. There was enough contempt without familiarity.

"What should we say?" I asked. I was the rookie, always looking for answers. Mr. Diaz, the other seventh-grade teacher and my fellow intern in the innovative Teachers For Chicago program, had been a substitute teacher in the past at different schools in the city. Donna and Mr. Callahan, the eighth-grade teachers, had put in years at this school. Their experience would be our guide.

"We should all say something," Donna said. "But the bottom line is they won't walk across the stage at the end of the year and graduate from eighth grade if they don't stop acting the fool. We are going on zero tolerance. No more clowning in the hallways. No more stealing from each other's desks."

Each of us took a piece of the problem to address. Donna would open the curtain with fire and brimstone. Mr. Callahan would appeal to their desire to move onward and upward. I would announce a peer tribunal to deal with the misbehavers. And instead of two lines, boys and girls, we'd walk single file through the hallways from now on in alphabetical order. We had fallen into such profound disorder so early in the school year that any attempt to impose order seemed reasonable. The principal threatened no more changing classes due to loud and unruly behavior in the hallways. The commotion disturbed the administrative personnel in the office, which is on the same corridor. They didn't like to be disturbed.

Donna had a brilliant idea to stop the thieving from the desks: When the students left their homerooms in the morning, they would turn their desks around so that the cubby holes faced in! That way, no one could get their hands inside to steal, destroy property or leave snotty tissues, trash, threatening notes or other unpleasantries. So simple. So brilliant in its simplicity. Those were things we rookies could not figure out on our own because we had no context and were surviving breath to breath. We were so overwhelmed by the complexities of teaching that we could not see the simple solutions.

We herded our students into the auditorium for the big bawling out.

Donna began with a prayer. She was a tall and striking African princess and a devout Christian, a Roman Catholic. Her voice rang like a bell. Her skin was the color of a Hershey bar, and her face shone with a light from within. Ask her how she was doing and she replied without fail, "I'm blessed."

Breaking all laws prohibiting prayer in school, we all bowed our heads and asked God to bless us and guide us and open our minds. She praised Jesus and warned of Satan (say-TAHN, she called him in private, with a devilish smile) and his sneakiness and lies, his trickery in leading people astray.

"These children act like shit in school," she told me, "but they are churchgoers and God-fearing."

As Donna wrapped up the prayer, a sudden ruckus broke out in the audience. Mr. Diaz's students leapt from their seats, shrieking and jumping around. First a couple, then more, then all. They flooded out of their rows and into the aisles, waving their arms and hollering.

Immediate thoughts: A rat! Roaches! Fleas! I backed up against the stage in case a rat ran out from under the front row. I was ready to jump back butt-first onto the stage with no part of my anatomy anywhere near that floor.

Donna went to investigate, a pissed-off look on her face. She was magnificent, queenly, disdainful. She moved like a fine sailing ship at sea to a row where a few students pointed out the trouble, covering their mouths in horror. I watched a flicker of disbelief, then amusement, dance across her face. Then, deadpan.

"Come on, now," she said in her teacher voice that cut through the hysteria, imposing order. "It's not like you never saw one of those before. Someone get the broom."

She headed back toward the stage and sidled past me after her discovery. My look said, "Well?"

"You're not gonna believe this," she said. "There's a turd on the floor."

"A what?" I said, disbelieving, as she had predicted.

"A goddamned turd," she said.

"Don't even look at me," I said, about to fall over with hysterical laughter.

"Don't you even look at me," she said out of the side of her mouth, walking past.

Somehow we managed to remove the feces, compose ourselves and deliver the lecture of the decade. Each teacher spoke. The ultimate horror—failing to graduate from eighth grade and go to high school—was repeatedly invoked.

But we also told them that we cared about them, that their success was our utmost concern. We implored them not to let their behavior prevent them from succeeding in school, not to let any foolishness get them off track.

We told them what we expected from them in simplest terms: Pay attention, do your work, do your best.

It was all true. We did care or we wouldn't have been there. We did care or we wouldn't have bothered. We did want them to succeed and we would do anything in our power to help them achieve success.

Would it have any effect? Impossible to say. Did they believe us? Their faces said they'd heard it before and it was bullshit then, so this must be more bullshit.

Later, after school when I had time to think about it, I wondered about the turd. Where had it come from? Who had left it? Was it imported from outdoors or actually deposited on the auditorium floor by its maker? Did a kid do it? A disgruntled adult? There was no shortage of suspects, that much was true.

I told my dad about it when we talked on the phone later. He'd seen many such oddities in his thirty years as a teacher. A kid once defiled a bulletin board outside his gym by adding a three-dimensional penis, molded from chewed chewing gum, protruding from the shorts of a basketball player pictured on the board.

The chewing gum sculptor was a one-shot deal. The Mad Crapper would strike again before the year was out.

Chapter 2

Welcome to the Neighborhood

When I said we'd fallen into profound disorder early in the year, well, that wasn't entirely accurate.

Disorder had existed at the school long before the year started. The same sort of disorder existed at other schools in our city and had for a long time. The kids ran wild. They swore, fought, refused to work. At assemblies they booed the principal. The only punishment was suspension, and that wasn't so terrible. As one of my students, Cortez, put it, "At least it's better than having to come up here and look at your ugly ass."

The school was a microcosm of the neighborhood. Pregnancy, drugs and alcohol were part of the life experience of children thirteen and fourteen years old. Parents had their own issues. Lives were consumed by the relentless stress and woe of poverty. Violence was omnipresent. The summer before, a serial killer had murdered prostitutes and left their bodies in abandoned houses. Gang shootings claimed players and innocents alike. Every family, it seemed, bore the scars of victims or perpetrators.

Cop friends tried to warn me, and public school administrators tried to downplay the extent of the chaos. The people who were trying to make a teacher out of me did not approve of excuse-making and held me accountable for a well-run classroom where children learned.

In reality, my classroom was just one deck chair on the *Titanic*. My school was just one of many poor-performing urban schools, trying to stay afloat as waves of social dysfunction crashed over its sides. But the philosophy of "no excuse-making" actually was the only way to proceed. It is what it is. Soldier on.

I believe my experience was more typical than extraordinary, more universal than unique. I understand the teacher shortage and why a third of new teachers quit after three years and half bail out after five years. No other industry would survive—or allow—such a personnel hemorrhage.

What was not typical about my experience was my background. As a newspaperwoman for twenty-five years, I had reported on Chicago's education crises long before the city's "school reform" effort grabbed the national spotlight. In 1987 former U.S. Education Secretary William J. Bennett described the city's public school system as "an educational disaster." The reform movement started two years later when Illinois lawmakers shifted power to local schools, putting local school councils in charge of their own budgets and destinies. Observers watched our experiment unfold with interest and guarded hope. If Chicago could turn its schools around, the thinking went, people anywhere ought to be able to fix their troubled schools.

In 1995 the state legislature took the final step, relinquishing control of the Chicago Public Schools to Mayor Richard M. Daley. They handed him a district in which only one-third of children could read and calculate at grade level. A bloated, insulated bureaucracy oversaw a small empire of aging, crumbling, patched-together buildings and more than a half-million children.

It would be Daley's greatest challenge. The success or failure of the school system would spell success or failure for the city itself. No industry would invest in an uneducated, untrained workforce. If the schools failed, the city's economic base would pull out, leaving the dropouts and crackheads behind. The nation's third-largest city would stumble and fall.

At the time, I was on the editorial board, the ivory tower from which newspapers dish criticism to individuals and institutions, and I wrote the following editorial, which appeared in the Chicago *Sun-Times* on May 22, 1995:

"Mayor Daley's complaining about state restrictions on money for the Chicago public schools is vintage whine.

His well-worn political spinning seeks to accomplish two things: reduce expectations of what the mayor can accomplish with the schools, and blame state bureaucrats for tying his hands. Sorry, mayor. We expect more from you now than ever before.

No one knows better than Daley that when the state offered him control of the schools, it was a classic case of "be careful what you wish for." Ended was his long tradition of lamenting Chicago's terrible schools with the luxury of no power to fix them. Well, now the problem is his to fix, and we are counting on him.

The Legislature will not provide any new money for Chicago schools. But we have confidence that the mayor will persuade legislative leaders to relax some of the regulations that hog-tie spending and encumber education. That must happen this week.

We expect the mayor to quickly appoint a qualified, five-member School Board. We expect Daley, as Mayor Rudolph Giuliani in New York is doing, to battle the financial bloat within the school bureaucracy. We expect him to make sure that those who lead the schools have one and the same interest: the students. We expect that the accountability now foisted on Daley will quickly move down the line. We expect schools to open on time in September.

Daley has several advantages. He has five years of school reform experience. He has bright stars of private industry providing expert advice and analysis. He has dedicated employees within the school system, and many models for success. He has an opportunity.

Nothing is more crucial to making the city a good place to live and do business than improving the Chicago public schools. That accomplishment will make Chicago shine for generations to come.

This period of enormous challenge is no time for defeatism or excuses. This is a time for Daley to show what he can do for Chicago. Roll up your sleeves, mayor. It's time to get to work."

Four years later, Chicago's schools had improved their finances, halted a disastrous cycle of teacher strikes, fixed crumbling buildings and put up new ones. Student test scores were beginning to improve. Yet Mayor Daley worried about sustaining the momentum. He asked, "How do you know that we set the foundation and it's not going to fall back?"

I believed the answer lay in the front-line troops, teachers, so I decided to take a dose of my own medicine. I followed the very advice I'd so stridently heaped on the mayor. I turned in my press credentials to become a teacher.

Of course, I thought I was pretty connected to "real life" by being a news reporter. I thought I knew plenty. I thought I was tough. I never imagined that a classroom of kids would bring me to my knees.

I learned that it is simple to raise taxes to replace crumbling schools and build new ones so children don't have to learn in closets and hallways. But it is very complicated indeed to compete for the hearts and minds of children in today's world, no matter how privileged the community or how dangerous the setting. Columbine taught us that. Urban schools have long known how very high the stakes are.

My students taught me more about hope and courage than a thousand Sundays in church. Leaving school to walk home after gunfire had spit bullets through the neighborhood, coming to school every day from homes wracked by drug and alcohol abuse or violence—they were my role models. As long as they kept coming back to school, so would I. Moments of grace and goodness sustained me as I struggled not to lose hope or the sense that God was with me and in each of my students. I never stopped believing that the fight, though not a fair one, was a good one.

For two years as I learned how to be a teacher, I sat on my back porch countless afternoons, trying to come down from the hysteria of the classroom. I'd listen to the cardinals and watch the leaves dance. I would replay the mind-boggling events of the day, and believe me, every day was mind-boggling. Always my eyes would return to the two icons that hang on the big linden tree in my backyard. They are terra cotta masks from Italy, a sun and a lion's head. Over time, I came to understand what they meant to me: hope and courage.

Those two irrational human qualities were the lifelines that lashed my chair to the deck, and my students to me and to the institution of school, and daily saved us all from sliding into a churning sea of despair and defeat.

All of this really happened.

Chapter 3

"Bring Two No. 2 Pencils"

I had no education credentials on paper, but the alternative certification program required only a bachelor's degree and a 2.5 overall college grade-point average.

As the nation faced a critical teacher shortage, alternative certification programs were popping up all over the place. Some cities were offering teachers free housing. Others were putting signing bonuses worth thousands of dollars on the table, luring teachers away from other cities. Recruiters invited fresh teaching grads to free room and board summer programs in hopes of enticing them to stay on and work in the fall.

The Teachers For Chicago program seemed like the perfect alternative path to teacher certification for me. It would cut through red tape at the state and city boards of education and requirements for entering graduate school. It would give me credit for as much of my undergraduate coursework as possible and keep required make-up work to a minimum. Most important, it would put me in a classroom immediately as a teacher, with a mentor looking over my shoulder and working with me daily.

The program would pay for my master's degree. I would earn $24,000 a year.

I mailed off my three-page application in October 1998 with three sets of "official" college transcripts, my original birth certificate and a money order for thirty-five dollars. Not a personal check, a money order. (What kind of deadbeats apply to this program? I wondered.) And three self-addressed, stamped envelopes. Three. OK. Whatever. I did it all. I sent it off with a prayer. I signed up to take the Basic Skills Test on January 9, 1999.

The day was freezing and snow-covered. It was still dark when I arrived at Bogan High School at 7 a.m. My main goal was to blend into the woodwork.

"I hope I pass this time," a woman said to me as we waited in line. "I failed it three times already."

Yikes, I thought. I should have studied. My memories of taking tests that required No. 2 pencils were dim indeed. This one was multiple choice. Timed.

I was nervous and not just about taking the test. Since my name and face were in the public eye quite a bit, and I know Chicago politics, I really wanted to fly under the radar. I didn't want anyone helping me or bollixing up my application because they didn't want me around.

It had been a long time since I'd gone anywhere before the crack of dawn but far longer since I'd taken a test that required two No. 2 pencils. Sharpened. They remind you of stuff like that. Teachers can be so doggoned prissy. "Sharpened."

But sure enough, one knucklehead showed up at the test with two brand new pencils that hadn't been sharpened.

"Where's the pencil sharpener?" he asked the teacher who was the proctor for our room. She glared at him with contempt, sucked her teeth and shook her head. There was no sharpener. He would have to borrow a sharpened pencil from someone else. (Someone who knew how to follow directions and come to school prepared for a test, unlike yourself, is what she really meant.)

We were all adults in that classroom, but I was struck by how the teacher treated the unsharpened pencil guy as a child and how some others in the room sort of went wolfen on him, casting yellow eyes on him, circling the vulnerable one who had showed weakness. I was back in school as sure as I was sitting at a wraparound chair/desk. It had been twenty-three years since I graduated from college, twenty-six years since I graduated from high school and thirty-eight years since I went to first grade, but the vibe was familiar.

Questions on the Basic Skills Test for teachers are like the under-$8,000 questions on *Who Wants to Be a Millionaire*. Any high school graduate who stayed awake in class ought to cinch it.

There was a grammar section, reading comprehension, an essay and—for me—the dreaded math. I am deficient in the math department, okay? Yet the most amazing thing happened. I experienced savant moments during which I somehow calculated the density of tin and solved a velocity question! I think this is what athletes feel when they're "in the zone." It's part motivation, part focus and it feels like flying.

Then came the essay: "Write a letter to the editor for or against requiring children to watch a certain television show as a homework assignment." What a snap! I'd won awards for editorial writing! I wrote a fiery letter opposing TV for homework. Students are overscheduled, I argued. Many have after-school sports and jobs. What if they don't have a television? What if it's broken or burglars made off with it in the night? If the show is that important, to be fair, the teacher should tape the show and let the whole class watch it together.

I left thinking that I would not want my own children to be taught by the woman who had failed such a simple test three times. And I felt sassy about my dazzling response to the essay question, the only part of the test graded by live human beings, educators.

The test results: Grammar, 100. Reading, 98. Math, 95. Essay, 80.

What the...?

When I got the test results, I thought someone spotted my name and sandbagged my writing score. But later I would find out the real reason I scored lower on the essay than the other questions.

Standardized tests do not reward creativity or flair in writing, they reward convention and conformity. Children are taught to write according to a certain formula. First they state what they will be saying. Then they break that into three main points, which they usually separate into three paragraphs beginning with "First," then "Secondly," and "Finally." Then they restate what they told you they were going to tell you in the first place. Then they are done. It is a deadly formula that produces moribund writing.

In the end the grade does not reflect ideas or the strength of an argument but spelling, punctuation and standard sentence structure.

It is a microcosm of the lowbrow nature of formulaic, lockstep, standardized education, structured curriculum and all the "do it this way" mandates that trickle down into classrooms, especially in low-performing schools.

Instead of minds and creative spirits set free, teachers and students alike are often caged in weak formulas and directives.

Some radicals in education believe our government does not want an educated population of free-thinking, articulate individuals but rather unquestioning worker drones to support our economy. Our obsession with standardized test scores would seem to support that theory.

A few weeks later I received a letter in the mail, addressed to me in my own hand with a return address stamped, "Teachers For Chicago." It was one of my self-addressed, stamped envelopes, coming back to me!

"Congratulations," it started. "You have been selected to interview for a Teachers For Chicago internship."

On February 22, I wore a sweater and pearls to my interview, and I had to show a photo ID. Once again I wondered, "What kind of deadbeats apply to this program? People who would send a surrogate to their job interview?"

But a minute into the interview I wondered whether I was the cheater!

Back in the fall, at the very first informational meeting, one of the Teachers For Chicago directors had mentioned a book called *Star Teachers of Children in Poverty* by Martin Haberman, a professor of education at the University of Wisconsin. Reporters pay attention to such details. I jotted down the title and ordered it from Borders. When it finally came in six weeks later, I read it. It was pretty good. Through more than 1,000 interviews with teachers in the pressure-cooker environment of urban schools, Haberman showed how "star teachers" think and react differently from those who fail in the classroom or become so disheartened they quit teaching altogether.

I was called into a small room, where two women sat at a round table. They took notes as we went along. One would ask the follow-up question while the other scribbled furiously. It seemed odd being on the other end of an interview.

And their questions! They were entire passages straight out of Haberman's book! The words coming out of their mouths described the exact scenarios he had detailed! They would start a question, and after a few words I knew exactly what would come next, not only how their sentences ended but how a "star teacher" would answer!

For instance, "Is it necessary for you to love all the children in order to be able to teach them?"

In Haberman's interview, the teacher answers, "Yes." It is the wrong answer.

The questioner keeps pushing. "I want to be certain I understand. You believe that love—not caring, respect, liking—but your love for the student is a prerequisite for you to teach him or her."

The teacher answers, "It's the best basis for teaching."

Wrong, wrong, wrong. In the classroom, love isn't all you need. Haberman's book said that response was "predictive of failure" because mutual love was regarded as the basis for teaching and learning.

"These expectations are shattered in urban classrooms when teachers find that they can only pretend to love every child, and that many of the children feel no obligation to pretend."

He concludes: "Stars relate closely to children and youth but do not intrude on their life space and do not use their relationship to resolve any of their own unmet emotional needs. Stars seek to create learners who will be independent and not need them."

And so to the question, "Is it necessary for you to love all the children in order to be able to teach them," I answered without hesitation. "No. Absolutely not."

Was that cheating?

A second envelope, addressed to me in my own hand, arrived.

"Congratulations! Your success in the application process has made you eligible for **possible** selection as an intern teacher in the 1999–2001 Teachers For Chicago program. The final selection and matching of 100 candidates to Chicago Public Schools and colleges/universities will take place in June."

The letter invited me to an "information session" at Roosevelt University, where we would register for a six-week Urban Teacher course. It would count as the first course in the graduate program for those who made the final cut.

"Because we believe in your teaching potential, this course is offered at no cost to you and allows you some additional experience before our final selection is complete."

The 200 semifinalists filled a big room at Roosevelt University—a wide range of ages and races and pretty evenly split between men and women. I was pleased to see many young black men in the group. In communities where absent fathers shadow the landscape, each could be an important role model in a school.

There were some kooky-looking people, one woman in a very dramatic hat, for instance, and sandals, even though it was quite chilly out and her feet were gnarly. I didn't recognize anyone from the Basic Skills Test or any previous contacts with the program. I noticed a woman in front of me with incredibly long hair that she twisted and wrapped into a bun, then secured with long sticks. Our paths would cross again.

The most intriguing line from our pep talk was this: "The first year is gonna be hell. The first month will be the worst experience of your life."

I signed up for the six-week Urban Teacher course at a small private university near my home. My class was balanced between men and women, black and white, and a scattershot of professions. Many already worked with children in preschools and parochial schools. A couple were long-time substitute teachers. There was a carpenter, a guy who ran a payday loan store and another who worked for a cellular phone company. A young woman just two years out of school had been working in television news, as a production or desk assistant. She wanted to become a teacher because "hearing all that bad news day after day was really depressing to me..." Reality check: If she couldn't handle bad news a layer removed, how was she planning to live in it day after day?

A guy who worked taking ads for a community newspaper said the $24,000 Teachers For Chicago salary would improve his family's financial situation. I decided it would be bad form to even hint at how it would destroy mine.

A federal housing muckety-muck had her sights set on teaching bilingual ed. Keith looked like he walked out of a rap video but was smooth as Marvin Gaye. Krishna had incredible energy and attitude. There was a lot of wisdom, too. Kimela, Celeste, Shenesia and Keisha had all taught for a long time without being fully certified. They seemed amazingly calm.

In six weeks we were supposed to learn the basics of running a classroom as well as the language of educators: "classroom management" (keeping order) and "methods" (how to teach) and "manipulatives" (math toys). We learned the different ways that children learn and the best ways to make knowledge stick. The most involved assignment was planning a four-week unit with daily lesson plans. Each of us presented one lesson to our colleagues. I went second, with a writing exercise from an eighth-grade poetry unit.

We had a fifteen-minute time limit. I passed out copies of a three-line Walt Whitman poem about looking out from a barn onto the countryside. I asked questions about perspective and descriptive language, about what pictures the poem made in their heads. Then I put on a tape of waves breaking on the shore and passed around a basket of shells and coral, lake stones and driftwood for each "student" to place on his desk for inspiration. I asked them to think for a few minutes about being at the beach. We brainstormed on different perspectives a writer could take (is the storyteller on the sand, in the water, under water, in the air, at sea?) and mood (is it a calm or wild day, is the calm deceptive because something menacing is under the surface or blowing in?). They wrote for about five minutes.

To my amazement every last person read his or her poem aloud. I was going to stop after a few, but they insisted on sharing—even our teacher! They didn't stand up at their desks either. Each came to the front of the room to "stand and deliver." A few of the poems were excellent, powerful and lean. I was moved by their effort and vowed to support every one of my fellow teachers-to-be to the degree that they supported me that night.

As the class wound down, people started receiving their assignment letters. Shenesia was the first. Then Kimela got one. Then Keith. Every time we came to class, more people had received letters. Theoretically, only half of us would be chosen, but looking around the room, I could name only three people who had not demonstrated that they could be excellent teachers.

Finally, a third envelope, addressed to me in my own hand, arrived.

"On behalf of the Teachers For Chicago Review Board, I am pleased to inform you of your selection as one of the 100 interns for the 1999–2001 program. Nearly 450 were interviewed for the 100 internship positions. We are confident that you have the potential to be an effective and successful teacher in the Chicago Public Schools. We look forward to helping you reach that potential in the next few years."

My assignment was an eighth-grade classroom at a public school less than three miles from my house, in the neighborhood where my husband grew up.

Chapter 4

My Assignment

We drove around the school block two times. There were two buildings—a beautiful old yellow brick school, built like a fortress in 1925, and another from the 1970s, a poured-concrete prefab shell three stories high. Built as a temporary solution to overcrowding, it had long ago outlived its intended lifespan. Over time the windows had become a cloudy opaque, impossible to see in or out.

Though it was near my neighborhood, it was like a different world. The physical barriers that separate the neighborhoods are a hill, a highway and skin color. In the school neighborhood, there were no white people walking around. Nearly every block had boarded-up houses.

"It's like a war zone over here," my husband observed of his childhood home.

I knew two people from my generation who were among the last whites to graduate from the school. I knew two others, who were in their 70s, who went to the school when the working class neighborhood was inhabited by Italians, Irish and other white ethnics. The houses were frame or brick, with big front porches.

My in-laws thought they would live there forever. Then, one day in the late 1960s, my father-in-law went out to cut the grass for the first time that summer. He came back in the house and asked his wife, "What are all those little black children doing on our street?" Like many other South Side Chicago neighborhoods in the grip of white flight, this tight-knit enclave became another domino toppled by fear. Unscrupulous realtors, fanning flames of racial hatred with the very real threat of economic loss, busted block after block. The whites sold cheap and moved out, some in the middle of the night because they were ashamed to face the neighbors they were leaving behind.

It was the beginning of a slide into wider economic disinvestment. Businesses moved out, too. Abandoned buildings started popping up, until it seemed that every block had at least one. The board-ups became havens for drug abusers and lairs for child molesters and rapists. Crime shot up. Gangs ran the streets and the parks. In recent years the only time I'd been to "the old neighborhood" had been to cover two gang-related child murders and once for a candlelight vigil for an innocent young victim of gun violence.

The neighborhood around the school, while poor, seemed relatively well-tended. A once-fine brick Georgian, on the corner right across from the school, stood abandoned, curtains flapping through broken windows. When I looked at it, I saw a social studies project.

The next morning, I returned to the school. I walked in a side door, past a security guard who did not question me, and introduced myself to the ladies in the office as "the new Teachers For Chicago intern."

"Hello!" they said, friendly and smiling.

They paged the principal, who came right away and took me into his office to chat. He looked weary. His eyes were bloodshot. Above his desk, tufts of pink insulation poked through a hole where ceiling tiles were missing. Other tiles were water-stained.

I asked for a copy of the school report card, a document that every public school in Chicago files annually. It lists statistics about individual schools' student population and achievement. He asked the secretary to find me a copy. The local school council president came into the school office, and he waved her into his inner sanctum to meet me.

I clicked off in my mind the political operatives in the neighborhood: U.S. Representative Jesse Jackson Jr. was the congressman, the Illinois state representative was Tom Dart, the alderman was Carrie Austin, and the incomparable Emil Jones Jr. was the state senator. There might come a time when I would call upon them for a service...

When I asked the principal for copies of the books I'd be using when school started in eight weeks, he sighed heavily and folded his hands on his desk. It wasn't that simple, he said. He wasn't sure what grade I'd be teaching. He was still working on his organizational lineup for fall. He assured me that my Teachers For Chicago mentor would be in touch and help me with the details of getting set up.

Chapter 5

The Farewell Tour

Monday morning I was jumpy as a cat, interviewing Paul Rodgers, the Bad Company singer who was taking the band on a final U.S. tour. He was in the Trump Towers in Atlantic City. I was at my desk at the *Sun-Times*. We talked about forty-five minutes.

After I put the phone down, I took the brown envelope with my resignation letter inside over to the office of the editor-in-chief, Nigel Wade, and quit my job. Afterward, I announced the news to my colleagues in the features department.

"Ladies and gentlemen, your attention please. I have something very important to tell you." They all looked up from their computers, stopped in their footsteps and looked at me expectantly.

"I'm leaving the *Sun-Times*. I'm going to be a teacher in the Chicago Public Schools."

They smiled. Sat there. They were waiting for the punch line.

"No, really!" I said. "This is for real."

They gasped. They burst into applause. A reporter in the *Homelife* section, got up and started walking toward the printer.

"Larry," I said in what I thought sounded like a teacher voice, "please return to your seat. You're up without permission."

I turned back to the room. "I will take questions now—but you have to raise your hands. Kevin Michael?"

"Where will you be teaching?"

"A public school in the Roseland neighborhood."

"Darel?"

"Don't you need a teaching degree?"

"I'll be an intern in a program called Teachers For Chicago, and I'll be going to graduate school. Details are in this memo, which I'm posting on the bulletin board."

My farewell column ran in my usual Friday space. I was not prepared for the stir it would cause. My colleague Richard Roeper put it in perspective: "Journalists always sit around the Billy Goat saying, 'One day I'm gonna go teach in the inner city.' They never do it. This is the first time ever."

Another fellow columnist, Neil Steinberg, griped, "The only way any of us can top this is to announce, 'I'm quitting to go wash the feet of lepers.'"

When I checked my voice mail around 10 a.m., it was full.

The first message was from a radio newswoman I'd worked with over the years. She was sniffing. "I read your column and I gotta tell you. You got me. I'm in the newsroom crying. It's beautiful what you are doing. I will desperately miss you, but I really respect what you are doing. If there is anything I can ever do, please call me. Congratulations. Good luck."

Calls clocked in every couple of minutes:

"I know what it's like to change careers after twenty to twenty-five years. Best of luck. You'll be great at teaching. Stay in touch." (political writer who became a consultant)

"Congratulations for having the courage to do this. All the best. Can you come on *Jay and Mary Ann* on Tuesday?" (TV producer)

"Blow me out of the water! It is a resplendently guts-bally thing to do. Will you come on the show Monday?" (radio personality)

"This is so cool! If you ever need a pediatrician, call me." (Cook County Hospital child abuse expert)

"Wow. I was absolutely floored to pick up the paper and see you. I never knew that was what you did. Call me!" (fellow Teachers For Chicago intern)

"Go for it! You may be disappointed. I hope you know what you're doing." (a Chicago Public Schools teacher)

I decided I was not available that day. I took my kids to our local park district pool and didn't return calls.

A guy came up to me at poolside and introduced himself. He was a banker, and he was on the local school council at my children's public school. "I wish I could do what you're doing," he said. "Good luck."

I was lying in the sun, reading, when another voice interrupted. "Baldacci?" It was the beat cop. He wanted to shake my hand.

"It's rough over there," he warned me.

"I know," I said. "But you tell your brothers and sisters to look out for me, all right?"

He promised he'd see me around.

Over the summer, he introduced me to other beat cops from the district.

"You doing this as some sort of undercover exposé for the paper?" one of them asked me. Another looked me straight in the eye, dead serious, and said, "Do you have any idea what you're getting into over there?" He acted like I'd just enlisted to go to Vietnam or something. It concerned him but also annoyed him. He saw me as a dilettante, a dabbler who was doing this for my own amusement.

I kept waiting for someone to write me a hate letter, which was business as usual at the paper. But no one did. Not a single person. Never had I experienced such a universal outpouring of good will or so many offers of "call if you need anything."

On WGN radio I talked about my life change, then listeners who had changed jobs at midlife talked about theirs.

Darla went from a corporate executive to a Ph.D. in anthropology, specializing in her Native American tribe. George went from corporate executive to college professor. Jim, a former truck driver, became a pediatric nurse. Linda helped her 49-year-old sister jump from an airline reservation clerk to a chef in Paris. "She's not coming back!" Linda said. Pat left a grocery store chain after twenty-four years to become a special education teacher. Janet worked for seventeen years in health care administration before becoming a pastor. John was in wholesale poultry distribution for twenty-five years, and he became a pastor too.

"When you hear that voice, listen," advised Janet.

A friend's father, a veteran teacher in the Chicago Public Schools, was listening.

"They're gonna eat her alive," was his sage reaction.

My last assignment for the paper was to review Bad Company's show at the World Music Theater. I took my twenty-two-year-old nephew. After I dictated the review over the phone, we moseyed backstage to pay homage.

Paul Rodgers' publicist girlfriend had told them that this was my last assignment for the paper, and all four had signed the page carrying my interview with the singer, which had run that day. To my great surprise, when I introduced myself, they jumped up and hugged me.

"It's so great what you're doing, going off to be a teacher and all!" they said in their cute British accents.

"Good luck, teach!"

"'Seagull, you fly.' Good luck!" Rodgers had written, quoting a lyric from one of his most beautiful songs. The summer before, I'd seen him play outdoors in Grant Park on Lake Michigan, and he'd performed that song in the golden early evening with seagulls wheeling and calling above. It was a moment that delighted the band—they were all pointing and grinning—as much as the audience.

Seagulls are disgusting scavengers, but I love them because they are a constant reminder in Chicago that the beach is near. Seeing them cut through the canyons of the city, following the river through the high-rises, always lifts my spirits. I regard them as a good omen, maybe because of that line from Jackson Browne's "Rock Me On The Water": "There's a seabird above you gliding in one place like Jesus in the sky."

Sometimes the gulls came in great numbers to residential neighborhoods, blanketing soccer fields or resting on light poles that stretch from both curbs, forming a seagull arch.

Seagulls, I would learn, also perch on garbage dumpsters in the parking lot of a certain school in the forgotten backwaters of my gleaming city on the lake.

Chapter 6

The Belly of the Beast

One Monday in July I went to the board of education to get my paperwork processed. Documents must be filed with the state and the city. There is a background and fingerprint check through the Illinois State Police. There are certificates to be obtained.

I had a folder full of paperwork—"official" college transcripts, birth certificate, letters from Teachers For Chicago. The drill is you traipse around from floor to floor, department to department, waiting for someone to help you, then get sent somewhere else.

After a couple of hours of this dance, I had obtained a substitute teaching certificate from the State of Illinois. This was progress! Finally, we made it to the right counter for city teachers' "processing." It sounded like I was about to become ham, and they even had one of those number machines like at the deli counter. I took a number and waited.

After about a half hour, a woman came and took all my stuff. She went away. She came back. She handed my documents to me, explaining that all the TFC interns were going to be processed the following week. I would have to come back then.

"But I'm here now. With all my stuff," I said.

Sorry, she said.

"Whose orders are these?" I asked her.

They came from the head of the substitute center. I tore over to her office, pissed that she sent someone to dismiss me rather than telling me herself or explaining why I had to make a second trip with ninety-nine other interns when I was here today, ready to take care of business now. Initiative, apparently, was not rewarded.

Her assistant was talking with two other women. I waited. Behind them, another woman hurried out of the office. After a couple of minutes, the assistant glanced up from her conversation and glared at me.

"Don't just stand there with your mouth hanging open," she hollered. "Say something!"

At that point, I'm quite sure my jaw dropped and my mouth was truly "hanging open." (Later, I'd learn that teachers who get in trouble for hitting and verbally abusing children are "reassigned" to desk jobs at the board of education, where they cannot abuse any more children, only adults—usually teachers.)

I need to speak to Ms. So-and-So, I said.

"She just left for lunch," the assistant snapped. "She'll be back in about an hour."

Suddenly, I got the picture. She sent the other woman to deliver her "come back next week" message that made no sense, then she quickly beat it out the door so she wouldn't have to deal with me or my paperwork. Nice move.

That sort of trickery was refined to an art form within the bureaucracy. The people who control teachers' paychecks, medical benefits, licensing and certification documents are experts at the dodge. They hide behind voice mail and pull all sorts of stunts to keep themselves unavailable.

The photo ID card guys, for instance. A bunch of interns went to get our ID cards only to find an empty office and a sign taped to the door: "No Photo IDs. Computer Broken." A group of us waited for someone, anyone, to ask if there was another way to get our ID cards. Eventually, two guys strolled in. They were well-fed and carrying big cups of coffee. They asked if we'd taken numbers and proceeded, in turn, to take our pictures and hand us our new ID cards. The machine was working fine!

The next week, I was back at the board on other business and had occasion to pass the picture room. The sign was still up and apparently the guys were out for coffee again. I told the frantic teachers waiting there to stick it out, and someone would come help them soon. It reminded me of Third World political shenanigans. You have to catch on to the game before you can play.

That first time I left the board of education feeling beaten. I couldn't believe I'd spent hours going from one counter to another, one office to another, and the only thing I had to show for it was a piece of paper from the State of Illinois allowing me to substitute teach for ninety days. The futility was one thing, but the insult of being given the slip and hollered at by the people who were supposed to be on my team was mind-jarring.

"If this is the board of education, why does everyone here act so stupid?" my nine-year-old daughter whispered to me at one dead-end.

She is a sweet and sensitive kid, and she had come along with the promise of lunch at our favorite Thai joint. In the course of the morning, she saw my spirits flag. After lunch, she offered to treat me to a Wendella boat ride, always a fun diversion but especially on such a splendid summer day. I accepted with pleasure.

Once we were out on the lake though, looking at Chicago's brawny skyline, I had what the Rolling Stones described as a "moment of doubt and pain." Our tour guide was pointing out the various radio and TV station antennas on top of the Sears Tower and the John Hancock Building, rattling off the call letters as if the antennas and their invisible signals were landmarks or monuments.

I had always been proud to be a part of an industry so powerful and important and so vital in people's lives. But now I was not a part of it at all. I was disconnected, floating on the lake in the Wendella, looking back. I was officially an outsider.

I wish I could say I had the good sense to sit back and laugh out loud at, "Don't just stand there with your mouth hanging open."

But instead I wept at my spectacular folly.

Chapter 7

Nesting

On the last Monday in July, I went downtown for the en masse "processing." I made it through without anyone shouting, "Don't just stand there with your mouth hanging open." This was progress, I supposed.

I had called my mentor for an update on which grade I'd be teaching. She said she'd call me back that Thursday but never did, and now it was ten days later and I still hadn't heard.

So I decided to relax, to "hakuna mutata" the situation, and to choose some juvenile fiction by African-American authors to read with my class, which, according to the school report card, would be exclusively African-American.

I read *A Girl Named Disaster* by Nancy Farmer and *The Watsons Go to Birmingham* by Christopher Paul Curtis. I read *A Lesson Before Dying* and *A Gathering of Old Men* by Earnest Gaines. I needed to expand my knowledge of African-American culture and history in order to weave it into my lessons. I was adrift but not idle.

I needed to talk to my mentor about some things. I needed a list of my students and their addresses so I could introduce myself, either in person or by a letter. I needed the textbooks I would be using in order to review the curriculum and plan lessons.

But in late July, when I stopped by school again, the principal emerged from behind closed doors to level his bloodshot eyes at me and tell me he still wasn't sure what grade I was going to get, but it would definitely be fifth grade or up. Two more teachers had quit, I later learned, and he had requested four additional Teachers For Chicago interns to fill the many empty spots on his organizational chart. The school's first experience with the nine-year-old internship program would place interns in eight of his classrooms. The poor man looked beleaguered. Running a school with 900 kids, eighty-nine percent from poverty-level homes, had to be tough. Student achievement was low: At third grade, eighty-six percent of the student body was below grade level standards in reading and seventy-nine percent was below grade level in math. On top of that, experienced teachers were bailing out right and left.

It was precisely the setting I wanted. The optimist in me, by virtue of a scant six weeks of education training, thought, "What if this turns out to be a turning point for the school? What if all these new people coming in with their energy and ideas make a difference?"

"I'm counting on you," he told me. I pledged my allegiance with a handshake.

"Put me where you need me," I told him. I sent up a simple prayer, "Thy will be done."

Since upper grades are in the old building, I went over to take my first look around inside my new workplace. The layout was exactly like my children's school, same vintage, built like an arsenal. Gym on one end, auditorium with a stage on the other. Two stories tall. The classrooms had high ceilings. The blackboards were ancient and in disrepair, likewise the bulletin boards.

The woodwork was dark-stained oak and there were built-in cabinets with glass doors. It reminded me of my house, which was built around the same time.

As I drove out of the parking lot, I noticed a demolition order nailed to the abandoned Georgian across the street. My cop friend from the park had started a new job with the abandoned house unit. He'd be a great resource to come in and talk to the kids about that rampant neighborhood hazard.

I put a dozen necklaces in a bag for a bulletin board on beautiful beads. I thought the artistry of the necklaces, modern and old, many African and Indian, might work as a writing prompt, thinking about people who might have worn beads like these in other places and times.

A new e-mail teacher friend, a TFC graduate, advised me to have the students work on the bulletin boards with me. She was just one of many teachers, total strangers, who sent me words of encouragement. Her first e-mail said this:

"I am glad to know there are still people interested in the Teachers For Chicago program. I still remember getting the phone call, letting me know I had been accepted. It was one of the best days of my life."

She said the man who was in charge of the program in her era was 'an inspiration to all 100 of us.'

"Whenever our determination faltered, we could count on him to pick up the phone and remind us why we were doing this. He always had positive things to say about our chosen career, and it was no secret how much he loved teaching.

"I am now entering my eighth year of teaching in the Chicago Public Schools. When I entered the TFC program, I had to take a fifty percent cut in pay, and to this day I haven't made up the difference. But I swear to you it was the best decision I've ever made in my life. I would do it all over again in the blink of an eye.

"The TFC program has helped me become a positive influence in the lives of many children. The mentoring I received through the program helped me through the roughest times, the times when I thought about quitting. But best of all, the program allowed me to do the thing I've wanted to do all my life, to become a teacher.

"Best of luck in your new career. I'm certain you will find that you've made the right decision. You will find that teaching may not be as glamorous as having your byline in the newspaper, but the rewards will be so much greater."

I was collecting angels, and I imagined them standing on my shoulders, like miniatures of the statues I'd seen at the Vatican, beautiful but fierce creatures with gowns and wings and giant swords. My imaginary angels were tiny versions of these stone warriors, but they had the faces of real people, known and unknown. All were encouraging me and protecting me.

Donna would often warn me to wrap myself "in the full armor of God." My armor had angel epaulets on each shoulder.

Standing tall in my angel corps was the Summer Fun Club, founded in 1978, which still returns to the "Sunset Coast" of Michigan each summer for our annual reunion. Our roots were the *Kalamazoo Gazette*. Over the years our summer digs moved among various houses in the town of South Haven. For two years we had a yellow frame house near the park, where our next-door neighbors were members of a band called Heartsfield. I married the drummer.

That year's reunion came two weeks before I became a teacher. On the beach, instead of reading a steamy novel or *Cosmo*, I spent days trying to crack the codes for the attendance book, to no avail. One evening, I returned to the house from watching the sunset to a blast of party horns and a shower of confetti. Those knuckleheads had thrown me a surprise party, the first of my life.

I got to wear a gold paper crown decorated with stickers of books and apples and chalkboards. There was a big chocolate cake frosted with an apple, speeches and gag gifts. Heartfelt good wishes showered upon me.

I could not fail!

Among the phone messages upon our return was one from my mentor.

"I'm pleased to tell you that you will be teaching seventh grade. Your room is 118."

My room. Seventh grade. How perfect. Just last year I channeled seventh grade through my older daughter. Civil War. Fractions. Pre-algebra. I could do that.

On the night before teachers were to report, I couldn't concentrate. I walked in circles. I had placed boxes of stuff by the front door, mostly books. I only had a couple of posters. I had no bulletin board supplies. I bought two little rugs at the grocery store for my "book corner," and I'd bring the overstuffed chair from our sunroom. I was like a woman about to go into labor, fussing about in a burst of energy to make ready for the baby.

Many teachers gave me the same advice: "Don't smile until Christmas." I didn't understand it and was positive I would never be able to do it. It's totally against my nature. I love to laugh. I shared this concern with my college advisor, when she called to remind me of the starting date for classes at Roosevelt University, where I would attend graduate school.

"Be joyful," she said. "A lot of these kids don't experience adults who are happy. They need it."

I couldn't wait to see their faces. I worked up my introductory rap and how I would assign seats using a card trick. I had notes on index cards on a clipboard. I had a couple of lesson plans, loosely structured like the radio talk show I hosted for two years. I was slightly organized. But I would be overwhelmed, I knew it, when I saw their faces, when I was face-to-face with the awesome responsibility of being their teacher.

I was joyful. I was terrified. It was a wonder I slept at all.

The next morning I made it to work in nine minutes flat. Driving east on 115th Street, I kept an eye out for who was up and about in Roseland at 8:15 a.m. A couple of boys on bikes, two stray dogs, an older couple out on a morning walk, the man carrying a stick in anticipation of stray dogs, a lady walking back from the store with a white plastic bag. I was thinking maybe I could ride my bike once in a while, though my cop friends begged me not to.

All the businesses were closed with burglar bars in place. The Knotty Pine Lounge, which had seen better days, was closed for good, an ancient "For Sale" sign hanging forlornly on the exterior. The small grocery store on the corner across from school was doing a brisk business. The marquee at school had this welcome back message: "Uniforms Mandatory."

Our day-long meeting was in the library, where I found all the interns sitting at one table with our mentor. Four would teach first, second and third grade in the new building; four others would teach fourth, sixth and seventh grades in the old building. I bet the first to quit would be Astrid, a fair-skinned blond with clear blue eyes who had some sort of emotional crisis at mid-day. Her upset, it turned out, was over being assigned to second grade. She was adamant about wanting to teach older kids. After a powwow with the principal over the lunch hour, she showed up in seventh, right across the hall from me.

"My sister!" I greeted her with a high-five. Astrid already had two master's degrees. She had been managing a Limited store in a suburban mall prior to Teachers For Chicago. She commuted an hour and a half each way from a distant suburb.

I spent a quiet lunch hour in solitude in my room, Room 118. I ate my turkey sandwich and drank my Coke and looked around at my new world.

It was painted seafoam green, which didn't look nearly as putrid with the dark woodwork as the pink in the library across the hall. The ceilings were so high the room echoed. A previous inhabitant had put up a lovely collection of Impressionist prints from a calendar. I needed to bring them down to eye level, as they were the size of postage stamps in the looming space of the classroom. I made a mental note to ask the art teacher to have the children make BIG art this year. It would take much to decorate this vast space.

My desk had four drawers; my chair was broken. The cupboards were full of junk I would never use, coated with years of dust. The next day would be a massive clean-up day. There were forty desks, which seemed excessive. There weren't enough electrical plugs. I wouldn't have a reading lamp in my cozy book corner unless I rigged up an extension cord.

Room 118 was blessedly on the west side of the building, so the morning sun wouldn't heat it to an oven by 9 a.m. Our windows looked out over trees and houses across the street instead of the parking lot. The downside of a first-floor classroom was being at street level, at greatest hazard from random bullets. I recalled an incident outside a school in which men firing guns ran right past the primary classes. The children and teachers could see them right outside the window.

Outside my window just then, as I ate lunch, were people out in front of their houses, watering grass, kids playing, guys working on a dead car with the driver's wheel up on a cinder block.

I said prayers inside Room 118. I thought about some of the things that were said in the meeting that morning, like how boys aren't allowed to wear earrings, but some must to gain safe passage on the way to school. A compromise was reached: Boys will clip their earrings to their shirt collars during school and be allowed to put them back in when it's time to go home.

A surprisingly high number of our students are in foster homes. We have to be especially sensitive to that, the principal told us. "You can't imagine some of the conditions these children come from."

In the temporary quiet of Room 118, I practiced names of my new colleagues—the blond-haired, middle-aged gym teacher who drove a motorcycle; the assistant principal; another teacher who knew my neighbor because their kids play soccer together on the soft green fields of Beverly, where no bullets fly. My neighbor later told me that this teacher was an attorney who bailed out of a downtown law firm to have hours that accommodate her kids.

Suddenly, it dawned on me that all the maps and the AV screen were pulled down. I wondered what was behind them.

I clomped and creaked over the wood floors to the far corner of the room and tried to roll up the AV screen. A huge chunk of blackboard, ancient, heavy slate, jagged and lethal, lunged forward behind the screen, threatening to slash right through it. Behind the slate was exposed brick, internal walls, vintage 1925. Behind the maps were unsightly chalk boards ruined by years of wear and subsequent efforts to cover them with contact paper and other sticky stuff. What a mess.

I had a word with J.T., the custodian who would save my butt daily, about the broken chair and the blackboard of death lurking behind the movie screen waiting to impale some kid. The assistant principal had me fill out a repair form. I had less faith in the repair form to produce results than I had that J.T. would hook me up.

The teachers I had tagged as the school's biggest rabble-rousers in the meeting earlier turned out to be the eighth grade teachers Astrid and I would work with on the upper grades team. Each of us would teach one core subject to two seventh-grade and two eighth-grade classes.

"I teach language arts, so that is mine," Donnamaria Gamble said. Danny Callahan, the other veteran, volunteered for math. "That leaves social studies and science," said Ms. Gamble, a tall, imposing woman with hundreds of braids, colorful speech and the grace of a natural leader. Our birthdays were the same week; she was a year older. Both of us were partial to dressing like teenagers when we felt like it. She looked terrific in her halter top, denim overalls and funky sandals.

"I love social studies, and I can't teach science," declared Astrid.

Shit, I was about to get stuck with science—ecosystems, energy, experiments. Panic rose inside me as an imaginary needle started to swing into a red zone beyond all that was new and overwhelming into the realm of that which was impossible.

"Look," I said. "I've been a news reporter for the past twenty-five years. I think we should each play to our strengths, and science does not play to my strengths. I would be very happy teaching language arts and I could teach an exceptionally rockin' social studies class."

Silence. Finally, Donna spoke.

"I'll tell you what," she said. "I'll take science because I'm halfway through my certification, and this will help me get done. You take language arts."

"Thank you," I told her, with heartfelt gratitude. It was the first of many gifts I would receive from the generous woman I would come to call a friend, a sister and my hero.

Leaving for the day, I noticed the abandoned house still standing. All the windows were broken now, and the demolition sticker was torn off. I stood out in the street and took pictures of the house from several angles. In a neighborhood where folks don't appreciate people nosing in their business, people have been shot over stupid things like that, I realized. I tried to put that thought out of my mind.

Nearby, a group of kids played football on the grass of the school. Their pink plastic football had no air. It was so deflated it was floppy and cup-shaped when they picked it up.

Two days to get the classroom ready, then the kids would be here. I went into hyperdrive! The first thing I put up was a framed picture of Steven Tyler, the singer from Aerosmith. It is a photograph taken on Milwaukee Avenue in Chicago. He is mugging and displaying the message on his sleeveless t-shirt, "Eat The Rich." That talisman went on the wall behind my desk for inspiration and protection.

I chose purple paper for my bulletin boards, and bought some African border at the teacher store. I hung up a Jimi Hendrix album cover, "Are You Experienced?" and yellow lettering: "Experience the Infinite Power of Words."

At the back of the room I taped up a poster of Chaka Khan and a poster from Hubbard Street Dance Company—a beautiful black and white Victor Skrebneski photograph of three dancers' legs balancing on a ball. Next to that, I hung on a nail a pair of my old pointe shoes. Finally, in gold letters left over from the banner at my surprise party, I spelled out "Stories Are Told In Music and Dance." There weren't enough letters to spell "through," so I made it "in."

I was filthy. I must have gone up and down the ladder a hundred times. The bookshelf was stocked with books on everything from gardening and architecture to sports and etiquette and Barbie, Hitchcock mysteries, self-help books, juvenile fiction.

As I was leaving, a fifth-grade teacher named Mr. Tyler, no relation to Steven, told me he came out of retirement from United Airlines to teach. "I clipped that column you wrote about becoming a teacher," he said, "and now, here you are at my school."

Chapter 8

The Seventh Graders Arrive

They were horrible. Horrible! It was a freaking nightmare. I had never seen kids act like that in a classroom with an adult present.

It didn't start out badly at all. The terrible part built slowly, like a running toilet that turns into a flood in the basement, accumulating slowly and silently, unanticipated and unnoticed until the hapless victim steps into knee-deep water.

A bell rang at 8:30 and I went out to the playground to greet my students, as instructed. I stood on the spot marked "118" and waited for my students to arrive and line up. I didn't know them and they didn't know me, so I didn't know who to look for or go after and round up. I simply established a beachhead on yellow numbers and waited and looked around.

It was loud and lively. Ms. Gamble and other veterans were able to greet kids by name and remark about how much they'd grown over the summer. Some older boys were playing basketball and girls were jumping Double Dutch. Parents were delivering small children to their teachers on the other side of the blacktop.

When another bell rang at 8:45, a security officer said "Let's go, let's go," and broke up the basketball game. Class by class quickly filed into the building. About a dozen kids stood near the 118 spot, looking at me expectantly.

"One-eighteen? Come with me," I said, and set off. We walked to the classroom without incident. So far, so good.

I had bought two decks of playing cards and put a card on each student's desk, face up. As the students entered our room for the first time, I handed each one a card. Find the match, I told them, and sit at that desk.

Students kept trickling in, but when it appeared twenty-eight was all we were going to get, I laid my welcome speech on them: "You hold the cards. How you play them is up to you."

For the rest of the day, every time I turned my back, kids tiptoed, crawled and slid to different desks next to their friends. All those new faces, my first day as a classroom teacher, I couldn't keep track of who was supposed to be sitting where. I wondered why the noise level kept soaring higher and higher. A poker game broke out in the back row.

But the main thing being "played," to invoke the vernacular of seventh grade, was me. "Be in charge. Establish control," I'd been told, over and over. The details of how to accomplish that had not emerged, though my mentor once mentioned something about how you had to "talk the walk." It was a prophetic malapropism.

The four upper grade teachers had agreed to change classes that first day, to jump right into the routine of changing classes. However, the lunch schedule delivered at mid-morning threw a wrench into our plans. We all got our homerooms back at second period, so lunches could begin at 11 a.m. Disorder thrives in confusion.

The afternoon would be long, I realized. There's a lot of day left when lunch is over at 11:20 a.m. I was surprised to learn that I was required to stay with my class in the lunchroom, and that there was no recess or break for the teachers.

In the afternoon, I had them write a first-day story. "A story has three parts"; I reviewed the three parts and gave them prompts for the beginning, middle and end. "When I woke up this morning the first thing I saw (heard, smelled) was ...

While I was walking to school I saw... When I walked through the school doors I felt..."

One boy wrote: "When I woke up this morning the first thing I saw was a dirty Pamper. When I was walking to school I saw a three-legged dog. When I walked through the school doors I felt hungry."

I loved that piece. It got us talking about all the things we can be hungry for: food, love, attention, knowledge and the next thing I knew we were discussing figurative versus literal language. For about ten minutes.

About an hour before dismissal, the students were restless, and the room was hot. Kids started hopping out of their seats, throwing paper balls, destroying their new rulers and pencils and hurling the sharp pieces at each other. They weren't doing it overtly, I'd just see things go flying through the air. I decided it was time for a washroom break.

Big mistake. That free-for-all brought both the assistant principal and the security guard running.

"All privileges are revoked!" the vice principal shrieked. She gave me a disgusted look as she stalked back to her office. Back in the room, I totally screamed at them. "If you ever embarrass me in front of my boss like that again, you will be sorry."

I called four parents after school to report that their children were disruptive in class. Pierre disobeyed a direct order and went AWOL—to another floor, no less—to visit his old teacher. I was relieved to learn later that Freddie, who seemed physically unable to remain in his seat and kept up a constant stream of chatter, was generally regarded as "crazy" by the veterans.

Astrid's seventh graders were horrid too. Her eyes were red and her nose was pink when we met after school to compare notes.

The kids were barely out of the building when I was thinking about tomorrow. The next day I would take their pictures and have them revise what they had written. Some weren't bad. There were several adequate spellers. We'd mount their portraits and first day stories on construction paper.

Tomorrow I'd tell them that I was testing them today, that the writing exercise that we did was the sort of work they are expected to do around page 230 of the book we hadn't even cracked. It was true—the part about the book. It was not true that I did it intentionally, but they did not need to know that.

That night, my daughter's eighth-grade basketball team played a game at our local park district field house. It was their fourth season, and I was their first coach. They'd come far, and they played as a unified team. It takes time to build a team. Seeing them helped my perspective tremendously. They were magnificent. They never looked better to me than they did that night. I was so exhausted I could not speak. I sat in the top row, shell shocked, my head resting against the wall.

On the second day, I went earlier. "I just need to be more organized," I thought. "The kids need more work to keep them busy." Teachers did not have access to a copy machine; copying was done by office aides on a two-day turnaround. If I handed in a copy order on Monday, I would get it Wednesday. We had no workbooks.

Four additional students arrived on day two. Our class was up to thirty-two students. So it was quite a large crowd the principal returned to me at dismissal because my class was unruly in the hallway. As he stood with his back to the window, lecturing my seventh graders about their poor conduct, I saw behind him, to my horror, two escapees from Room 118 outside our windows, hamming it up behind the principal's back to the amusement and delight of the others.

If I had been fired on the spot, I would not have been surprised.

I stayed until 5 p.m. working in the classroom and organizing my card catalog of students and their home phone numbers, which I realized I would be using nightly to call parents about their children's dreadful behavior.

On the third day, a girl came up to me in third period and said, "I don't feel good. I think I'm going to throw up," and proceeded to barf in my book box on her way to the trash can. In most classrooms, a throw-up incident would be the most traumatic event of the day. But in Room 118, it barely made a ripple. Hardly anyone even noticed. I dragged the book box out into the hallway and told three different office personnel in the course of the afternoon that I needed a janitor. No one ever came. I ended up cleaning off the books myself after school.

As I knelt down in the hallway, wiping off the books with a wet sponge, the vice principal walked past. She was a real miser about books, and I respected that. She alone held the keys to the "book room."

"Are you throwing those out?" she demanded. No, I said, someone puked on them this morning and no one ever came to clean up the mess. That got rid of her quick.

I knew in my head that the goal of seventh grade is to derail the train not just the first day but every day. I knew in my head that teaching is like the Ike and Tina Turner version of "Proud Mary."

"We never do anything nice and easy. We only do it nice...and rough."

But it was already so hard. Even the parts that appeared simple turned into major disasters for the uninitiated. I was told to hand out books, so I handed out books without writing down which kid had which number book! Even a no-brainer like taking attendance devoured a tremendous amount of time every morning, especially with the late arrivals and new people showing up every day. And I still hadn't figured out that absent children got a double slash mark in the square for that day, while tardy kids got a capital T. All anyone told me is that attendance books are a legal record and mine had better be in perfect shape when it was handed in or else! The only thing teachers are required to remove from a burning building (or during a fire drill) is the attendance book. It is some sort of holy grail in education circles. Not until the next year would I come up with a good system for my attendance book: Write it in pencil first. If a kid is absent, make one slash mark, which you can easily turn into a "T" if he shows up late. If he never shows up, make it a double slash the next morning. At the end of the month, balance your book, then ink it in. Use black ink. Redline the kids who never show up and the kids who transfer. Keep your red lines going month after month during the school year. And never—NEVER— let your mentor do your attendance book for you.

My student with autism arrived on day four. One good thing was that he seemed quiet and kind. Another good thing about Nelson was that he had a full-time aide who might help in the classroom.

I put the two of them at a table of four other good kids, but later realized they might be a stabilizing influence with borderline kids. Perhaps the close proximity of an adult would make the difference between total chaos and mere disorder. Nelson sort of went off into Tai Chi sometimes, but he seemed to be a gentle, inquisitive, conscientious soul. Which is more than I can say for his mostly awful classmates. The irony of the disabled child being the model child dissolved me into tears as I tried to describe my day to my husband.

"What do they do that is so bad?" Artie asked me.

They talked incessantly. They shouted to be heard over the talking. They didn't do their work. They got up out of their seats without permission and wandered around, touching and bothering each other on their way. They shouted out questions and comments, including, "This is stupid." Any little ripple set off a chain reaction. Someone passed gas and everyone leapt from his seat fanning the air and jumping around. They threw things. They hit. I had broken up two fist fights already. They yelled out the window to their gang-banger friends and relatives, who gathered outside at dismissal time. They swore like sailors. One of my kids called Astrid a bitch.

Student number thirty-four showed up the following Monday. I asked him where he'd been the first week of school and he told me, "buying school supplies." It seemed like a weak excuse at the time.

When student number thirty-five arrived, I gave him my chair and sat him at the activity table. Later, after everyone left for the day, I sat in my chair and put my head down on the activity table and cried. I felt like the old woman who lived in the shoe. I had so many children I didn't know what to do. I was still learning their names: Tyrese, Sherika, DeVille, Kyisha, Pierre, Destinee, plus twenty-nine others in my homeroom alone. More than a hundred other students called me their English teacher.

Out of all those children, Pierre was the first name I learned because he had a larger than life persona. Pierre was in seventh grade on some sort of "waiver," after failing the summer bridge program that determines whether a borderline child can be promoted. Five of my students were in seventh grade on these waivers, all doing poorly, all discipline problems. But Pierre was above and beyond. A typical conversation:

"Pierre, please sit down where you belong and stop talking."

"I'm not talking. Why don't you ever say anything to anyone else. I swear I hate you, you ugly..."

Then there would be some chair slamming and posturing, and he'd mutter and continue to pout.

But the other side of Pierre was that once he settled down, he did all his work. He was a good speller. He wanted to be involved in everything—spelling bee, messenger, cheerleading—he was always offering to help with odd jobs, and constantly engineering ridiculous scams to get out of the classroom to wander about the building. Some teacher or principal always "needed to see" Pierre.

He reminded me of an alcoholic who starts each day with the best intentions but something along the way trips them up and they start to sink in the quagmire of self-defeat, unable to pull themselves out and worst of all, in complete denial.

Chapter 9

Getting to Know Them

The end of the week found me standing in my backyard, watering the grass. Back and forth. Back and forth. I watered the grass for forty-five minutes, just trying to come down from the hysteria of my classroom.

Nothing had gotten better. There were a few minutes each day when things seemed to be clicking along, then everything would fall apart.

People say, "When I was in elementary school there were fifty kids and one arthritic nun in a wheelchair, and you could have heard a pin drop..." Why couldn't I do that?

Why couldn't I control kids who'd been running their own lives for years even though they were only twelve? When I called their parents, they said they couldn't control them either and asked me what they should do.

DeVille, one of the worst cut-ups, shout-outers and insulters of his peers, criticized me for failing to control the class.

"Why do you want to be controlled?" I asked him. "That sounds like a slave mentality. You are all old enough to control yourselves. You need to control yourselves so that I can teach and you can learn."

Was there a racial element? Was a white woman in this setting destined for failure? Did black children need to express their contempt for white authority in the same way all children this age have to express their contempt for all authority? I'd heard gossip that some veterans at the school had questioned "who they think they are that they can come in here and teach our children," implying that the four white women interns had no business here. Children pick up on attitudes the way animals sense fear. Was my class feeling empowered because they knew my backup was weak?

And where was my backup? What were the consequences? Everyone I sent to the office bounced right back in. There was no detention. There had been no suspensions, even for fighting. I was beginning to think "alternative" schools for poorly behaved students were a myth made up by the board of education. Was my school an alternative school and no one told me about it? Was every student retained, no matter how terrible the behavior, to keep the federal money pouring in? Schools receive federal dollars and USDA breakfast and lunch funding for every student whose family income is below a certain level.

All good questions, but ones I could not resolve. These were issues I needed to discuss with an experienced hand, but I hadn't seen much of my mentor. I felt like a prisoner in solitary confinement, thrown into a cell and forgotten. I was lucky to get to the bathroom in the course of a day.

I started to get the idea that things were less than perfect elsewhere in the school. I heard that an intern who had a first-grade class called it quits after two weeks.

"I didn't know it was going to be this hard," she said before heading out the door. Before trying teaching, she'd been a cop for seventeen years.

Another intern was mysteriously missing in action from our school, though she was still showing up for our college classes. Later, she said she'd transferred to another school. She didn't offer the reason.

Astrid and I talked after school every day. She was only in her twenties, a sassy girl with multiple piercings and a tattoo, so I expected her to be tougher or bouncier than me. But many days she plopped down in the middle of the hallway, spent, after the children left. By the same token, my age and life experience were not helping me be tough or bouncy. Ramona and I were equally confused, exhausted and overwhelmed. Every morning we marched in like soldiers, hopeful and brave. By afternoon we felt like utter failures. I'd hear her voice rising higher and higher in the afternoon as her students spiraled out of control. She had more than a few who acted completely demented, running out of the classroom as if in a jailbreak. Students got "written up" and referred to the office for their misbehavior. Their parents were called to school and the kids were bawled out. They'd be back in the classroom in no time. My voice was getting lower and lower. It was raspy from shouting. I had to sing an octave lower at church. I wondered if I had permanently damaged my vocal cords.

We logged a minor success when my seventh graders actually read a complete story in our reader. We used the "round robin" method, criticized by educators, because the children wanted to do it that way. They were familiar with reading that way. Different people read passages, even Nelson. The room got real quiet. They were curious: Could he read? Yes. Quite well. I had to be extremely specific with him, but he asked good questions and liked to be included in classroom activities. He was a good communicator for someone labeled autistic.

Our story was cute, about a boy who tries to impress a girl he likes by pretending he knows French. Andre, who was pleased to learn he has a French name, asked me if I would teach him how to speak some French. I told him *"oui"* and that I'd bring a book so we could start tomorrow.

Bonjour! They arrived to find the desks rearranged for the third day in a row with assigned seats. I created tables one through five, plus The Guys In Front (TGIF), who needed extra supervision.

There was a tsunami of angst, hysteria, bellyaching and acting out over seat assignments, kicking of chairs, swearing. Pierre was strutting around with his hands on his hips shouting, "I am not going to sit next to Destinee, and you know I can't get along with her and we're just going to get in a fight…" He threw a chair! It was such ridiculous behavior that I laughed out loud. "Sit down and stop your noise," I told him, sounding exactly like my mother. He huffed and puffed, but eventually picked up the chair and put his butt in it.

Once I got them quiet, I laid down the New World Order: This was how it was going to be until I decided otherwise, because I was the queen of Room 118 and what I said was law. I told them about the conference forms I had copied at Office Depot the night before, which were ready to go home with anyone who could not behave, requesting a parent conference the next morning before school.

"You know your parents will not be happy when they hear what's been going on in here," I informed them. Their looks told me they knew that.

Overall, I'd say better cooperation, maybe five percent. But the sporadic calm was so tenuous, so elusive. It only took one little thing out of the ordinary and a tornado would engulf the room, pulling everyone up in its swirling chaos.

Our new dismissal procedures caused a real tizzy. At 2:15, the blinds went down to prevent any gang signifying out the classroom window. With their backs to me, I couldn't be sure whether what was going back and forth with people on the sidewalk was an innocent wave or a Gangster Disciple sign, and I wasn't taking any chances.

Table by table, depending on who was quiet, they would go to their lockers. Then they placed their chairs on top of their desks and lined up.

Problem was, the chairs were molded plastic with metal legs, and they slipped and slid off the desks with the least provocation, crashing onto the wooden floors. Thirty-three chairs, and I'd bet twenty-five of them ended up back on the floor, some purposefully for the sheer pleasure of creating noise and disorder. The din was incredible.

At the end it got really ugly. Chairs crashing, kids yelling, running, hitting each other. I jumped up onto Freddie's desk and demanded their attention.

Eric continued running his mouth, right next to me.

I jumped down off the desk, landing square in front of him. "Stop it!" I screamed in his face. That shut him up for about three seconds, then he started talking again. I was so mad I thought my head might explode, like in that movie *Scanners*. That was not a good mental state for a teacher.

I climbed back on Freddie's desk.

"No one's leaving this room until you are all quiet," I told them.

The room was sweltering. The minutes ticked by, 2:35, 2:37. People started whimpering they had to pick up siblings, had to get home. The worst provocateurs waged the greatest protest. I put my finger over my lips in the universal sign for quiet. At 2:40, they were quiet. We formed lines in the hallway and started walking to the doors. I made them stop twice, once to wait for some little kids to pass and once out of sheer spite.

I despised them. Reeling from the day, I packed my briefcase and headed downtown for my college class. Being with adults in air conditioning was like a cocktail party.

Chapter 10

Al Gore Visits the Billy Goat

Thursday night I met my friend Mary Mitchell, my former protege and fellow columnist from the *Sun-Times*, for a beer at the Billy Goat, the legendary media hangout immortalized in the *Saturday Night Live* "Cheeseborger, no fries, chips" skit. It was my neighborhood bar, located between the *Sun-Times* and the *Chicago Tribune*. It was the only bar I ever felt comfortable walking into alone, because I always ran into people I knew. I felt good today, as if things had gone better, though they really hadn't that much. Then I realized what it was: Today I didn't break up any fights!

And talk about a new perspective. Billy Goat's bathrooms, which I had in the past tried to avoid at all cost, seemed sparkling clean to me. They had soap. I washed my hands three times before pulling up a barstool next to Rick Pearson, political writer of the *Tribune* who I'd worked with in the early '80s at United Press International.

"Don't look now," he said, "but Al Gore is going to walk through that door in about five minutes."

Sure enough, a little after 7 p.m., the vice president of the United States stopped by to press the flesh, surrounded by a dozen cameras and the usual secret service detail.

As Gore made his way down the bar shaking hands, I introduced myself as "Leslie Baldacci, Chicago Public Schools teacher."

"Oh!" Gore said, "any relation to Representative Baldacci of Maine?"

"No," I said. "Neither to David Baldacci, the famous author."

"Joe's mother has a restaurant in Maine called Mama Baldacci's," Gore informed me.

"That's cute," I said. "I have a daughter named Mia, and I always thought that when I opened my restaurant I'd call it Mia's Mama."

He laughed, "That's great!" and moved on.

I knew then that Al Gore would not be elected president. In seven years at the knee of the master, he had learned nothing.

Here's what Bill Clinton would have done if someone dropped the million-dollar sound bite "Chicago Public Schools teacher" in his lap:

Clinton would have gripped both my hands. His eyebrows would have shot up and he would have locked those steely blue eyes on mine. "No kidding!" he would have said. "How has your school year started off?"

And as soon as he heard what a disillusioned first-year teacher had to say about my seventh graders who can't read or capitalize "I," their horrible behavior, our torn up, worn out books, their disrespect for themselves and others, he would have pulled up a barstool, ordered a Diet Coke and spent some time listening, questioning.

Even if he had heard it a thousand times in a thousand other cities and knew it by heart, he would have listened because it had to do with the top concerns in the country, education and violence. It was a golden opportunity to make nice with a member of a powerful labor union that happened to be the top contributor to Democratic party coffers in Illinois. He would have seen the opportunity to connect—not only on a personal level but in a way that would burnish his image on CNN. An aide would have gotten my name and the name of my school and there would have been follow-up, maybe even boxes of the Houghton Mifflin spelling and English books I coveted with all my heart. All of that would have been crystal clear to Clinton in one split second.

And that is why Clinton, though flawed in so many ways, survived, and why Al Gore didn't get elected.

I even gave Gore a second chance. I got a piece of paper and a pen and made a second pass, asking for his autograph for my students. I slipped when I made the request, calling them "my kids." Uh oh. Bad sign. I simply refused to fall in love with those abusive little bastards. Gore signed the paper down at the bottom. Later, I wrote at the top, over his signature: "By order of the Vice President of the United States:

All students must behave for Mrs. Baldacci." I put it in a frame and hung it in the classroom.

"How do we know you didn't forge that?" Joseph asked.

"Why don't you go ask Ms. Gamble who she saw on the Channel 5 news last night and again this morning, shaking hands and talking to the vice president of the United States," I told him.

Later, after I'd sent Cortez to Donna's room to collect papers, he returned in a dither and blurted out to the class, "It's true! Ms. Gamble saw her on TV with the vice president!"

By order of the vice president of the United States, behavior in my room improved about two percent.

Chapter 11

The Kids Are All Right, but the Teachers Are Wrecks

Most of the interns showed up for college classes sick. They had god-awful colds, bronchitis, lost voices, impetigo. I knew it was going to be grueling and made a point to put myself to bed at 9:30. I slept like the dead. I got up at 6:00 and swallowed huge megavitamins. I packed a healthful, protein-packed lunch with a juice. I drank lots of water. I was constantly moving around, constantly on my feet. It was like working outdoors or training for the Olympics. For a while, I lost a pound a day, even though I ate three meals.

What did I have to show for it? Eye infection, yeast infection, pimples, diarrhea, the result of stress and filth, with no opportunity to wash your hands. I made a note to myself to check whether Wet Wipes came in anti-bacterial. I got dirtier at school then I did working in my garden. Whenever I washed my hands in the teacher's bathroom, which had no soap, the dirt from my hands made a dark trail down the drain. I showered in the morning and again as soon as I got home because every inch of me was sticky with a coating of sweat and dirt and chalk dust.

School had started August 24, the earliest ever, and summer was in full bloom. On four days early in the school year, the outside temperature soared into the nineties. Our western-exposure classroom in the afternoons was so hot I worried some kids would faint. Racquel had to sit in the hallway one afternoon, she was so woozy. Montorio brought a fan from home, bless her heart, but loud arguments erupted because people would stand in front of it, hogging the air.

With work coming into the pipeline, I had a lot of papers to correct. It took hours, I learned. It could eat up a whole weekend.

Experienced teachers correct papers on their prep periods and during lunchtime because that's when they have the energy to do it. After school or at home the task is much harder to face. You carry the same folders of uncorrected papers back and forth to school day after day. New work piles up. Correcting papers and lesson planning account for an extra day of work each week for which teachers are not paid. Maybe that's why worksheets, while not a "best practice" in education, are preferred by many teachers. They are quicker and easier to grade than essay-type papers or projects. Unfortunately, they are also easier to complete since they usually require students to supply only factual information, not higher-level interpretive or evaluative thinking.

I had final drafts of the "First Day" story, a twenty-word spelling test and a proofreading worksheet, a pile of stuff. But the greatest surprise was not how much time it took to correct the papers. Suddenly, the curtain was yanked back to reveal who was working and who was not. I saw I had been hoodwinked.

Some students beguiled me with their social skills into assuming they were good at schoolwork. The Bible-reading captain of the safety patrol turned in not a single thing—not even the spelling test he took with me standing right there. Other well-behaved students could not spell "hello" or capitalize "I."

However, Pierre turned in everything and did each part very skillfully. Kyisha, who wore her attitude on her sleeve and loved to have the last word, completed her work quickly and well. She was a prolific writer. Sherika, who said she was proud to be "ghetto," was practically illiterate. I sent a note home asking for a conference that week. It was not returned. When I asked where it was, Sherika said her mother was "out of town."

"My brother is taking care of us," she said. He was fourteen.

Sherika was worldly beyond her years. In the lunch line, some girls were looking at a magazine ad, one of those "Got Milk?" pictures, featuring Tyra Banks with foamy white milk on her upper lip.

"I'm not even going to say what that looks like," Sherika observed with the jaded countenance of a twenty-dollar hooker, pointing to the white substance. She was twelve years old. I would later learn more about her mother's going "out of town."

I moved Destinee, who turned in nothing but the spelling test, to another table. She and Pierre had a fight, as he had predicted. Destinee kept her head on her desk all morning because she didn't like her new seat.

"You owe me assignments," I told her. "Do your work, and you will get your privileges back."

I couldn't figure out how Darnell, with second-grade test scores, made it to seventh grade. He had not been tested for special needs, so he received no remedial help. He was just there not understanding anything. So he threw things and broke things and cut up. I spent more time working with his group than any other. It was never enough.

I phoned Eric's mother. He, too, turned in not a single bit of work. He never stopped talking. His mouth ran constantly; he never knew what we were doing or even made a pretense of being involved. If his book was on his desk, it was closed. If his work was on his desk, the page was empty. He had the highest standardized test scores of anyone in our room, nearly two years above grade level in reading.

"I don't know what to do about him," his mother said, breaking down in tears. "Since his father died I can't control him."

I'm very sorry, I said, I didn't know. When did his father die?

"Four months ago," she said, "from cancer."

Jesus Christ! Isn't that something a classroom teacher should know? How could a kid go through that and not have a single note in his file? How could no one at school be aware of it? How could his classroom teacher not be informed? No wonder the kid couldn't concentrate! No wonder he couldn't keep still! How could he care about school when school didn't care about him? His mother, beside herself with grief, had two other teenagers at home. She was clearly overwhelmed. "I just don't know what to do," she wept. I asked Donna about it in the afternoon, when we went to the office at the same time to pick up our first paycheck of the year. She assured me that over time, as I got to know the kids better, information would come to me through them.

"Some of it you'll wish you didn't know," she said, shaking her head. "Don't expect to get it from the office."

I regarded my paycheck: $633.45 for two weeks' work.

"How much of a pay cut did you take?" she asked me.

"Two-thirds," I answered.

"Shit, Baldacci, what for?" she wondered.

"Because a voice called and I answered," I told her. It was the first time I'd admitted that out loud to anyone outside my family and a few close friends. Although I did not know her well, I felt she would understand. She jerked her head and looked at me in surprise. Then a smile spread across her face.

"My sister," she greeted me, as if meeting me for the first time.

I was still trying to figure out what these kids could do besides shout out wisecracks, pick fights and complain about school. So I got a few other little projects off the ground. Each one took a great deal of organization and gathering of materials. One was a writing assignment, a for-or-against people being allowed to own exotic pets. I copied newspaper articles on a toddler killed by a python and city workers hunting for an escaped serval.

Also, the date 9/9/99 was coming up and I wanted to do something special to mark the date. After searching a couple of branch libraries, I found a CD of Beethoven's Ninth Symphony in D Minor. I spent ten dollars on Sunny Delite, paper cups and cookies and shoehorned the lesson in between lunch and gym.

First I talked about Beethoven and his genius and his tragic deafness and about him writing this famous symphony, which was inspired by the French Revolution. I tossed in a bit about the revolution and compared it to the American Revolution and the civil rights movement.

I handed out art paper and asked them to listen to the tape and to draw a picture of what they thought Beethoven was trying to say in music.

It was fun at first. They drew and chattered quietly. By the beginning of the second movement, they were loud. By the end of the second movement, they were out of control. Darnell was swiping cookies by the fistful and guzzling Sunny Delite straight from the bottle. The empty plastic jug was stomped on the floor. Kids were whining and complaining that they didn't get any.

I stopped the music, snapped off the lights and yelled at them about their behavior.

"It's a shame that we had something nice going on here, and a few people had to go and ruin it," I growled. "That is terrible manners to drink out of the bottle and grab up as much as you can when these treats were for everyone to share."

I was fit to be tied. All that preparation for a big fiasco. In other classrooms, kids were sitting at their desks quietly filling out worksheets. We tried to do something creative and it was a train wreck.

But to my great surprise, when we looked at their drawings, Kyisha had sketched a crowd of people carrying signs that said "Freedom." Someone who talked non-stop the whole time had drawn an elaborately detailed picture of a conductor leading a symphony orchestra.

C. C. amazed me by drawing the outside of a concert hall and struggled to write the words, "The celebration is in here." It took us several minutes of hard work to sound out the spelling for "celebration." He substituted the word "and" for "in." I had just found out that day, when the special education teacher appeared in our doorway, that C. C. and three other students went every morning to pull-out reading class. Fortunately, one of my college courses that semester was about special-needs children.

The poor communication, along with the isolation, had me feeling displaced and confused. In the classroom, I felt awash in a swirling current of bodies and noise, like being in a Lotto machine or a clothes dryer. People came and went. It was not until later that I even realized I had one-on-one time with students, that we managed a few minutes of connection in the middle of the action around us.

Later, when the dust settled, snippets of conversation replayed in my mind.

"Where's Melvin today?"

"With his parole officer."

"Ms. B., can you skate?"

"You bet. I played ice hockey with boys in college."

"What rink do you go to?"

"I roller skate in my neighborhood on the street, but I ice-skate at Mount Greenwood Park. You could take the 111th Street bus and meet me there on Sunday afternoons."

"This Sunday?"

"No, it's too warm outside for ice. Later this winter, though."

There was Nelson's melt-down over lunch.

"I'm allergic to all vegetables, especially corn."

He was seated with his lunch (ham slice, roll, fruit). Later, he saw some kids had chicken nuggets and he wanted that instead.

"No, the cafeteria ladies already made you a special no-vegetable plate. You can't ask for a second favor."

He got mad and threw the ham lunch in the trash.

"I can see you are angry. If you don't like the school lunch, you could bring your own lunch to school. Or you could trade with someone else who likes ham better than chicken nuggets."

That was too much. He lost it and had to "go upstairs" for a while with his aide.

My TFC supervisor from downtown stopped by. She gave me a pep talk about how I have to find ways to reach every child and expressed neither outrage nor hope that my enrollment would drop.

As I left school guys were sitting, drinking on the school steps. As I drove past, one yelled, "Fuck you, bitch!"

It occurred to me I hadn't seen a single squad car in our "safe school zone" so far.

That night at graduate school, I listened enviously as Michelle, who had waist-length hair that she wore in a twist secured by two chopsticks, told us that she and her fellow intern have their fifth graders competing in a good behavior contest, how they are now perfect citizens in the hallways and classroom. It confirmed my suspicion that I was a complete failure.

Chapter 12

Violence

In places where the pen is not mightier than the sword, a pen can be stripped for parts and made into a sword. Violence is always near.

Certain acts are sure-fire ways to set something off: talking about someone's mother, for instance, or calling someone "bald-headed." The arrival of a new student, boy or girl, guaranteed a fight so the fighters could assert their dominance, let the new kid know who was in charge. Violence was often a reaction to violence.

One Tuesday morning, the math teacher smacked Melvin around in the hallway outside my classroom before third period. I could hear the slap upside his head as clearly as I heard Tyrese and Jeremy landing punches on each other earlier that morning, when I broke up their fist-fight in the hall outside the gym.

"You can't do that, man," Melvin griped loudly. His face was tight, ashen, and his body was tense and tightly coiled, boiling with anger as he walked into my room.

Within five minutes he had broken a pen into a sharp, jagged plastic point and stabbed Robert in the hand. I gave Robert a Band-Aid and turned the pair over to the security officer, who by the grace of God was passing my classroom.

Earlier, I had been too consumed with the task of getting my home-room from outdoors to their lockers and the classroom to have dealt with Tyrese and Jeremy, who were rolling on the floor punching each other's lights outs near the gym.

My technique for breaking up fights was this: Lean in close, but not too close, lightly balanced on the toes to facilitate a dodge or jump back if necessary. "BREAK IT UP RIGHT NOW. RIGHT NOW!" had worked so far. The blows came fast and furious and I had no desire to have even one land on me. It was a poor technique. I would not make it through the school year unscathed.

I told the math teacher that Melvin had been so angry about being knocked around that he stabbed Robert in my room.

"He told you that?" the teacher said.

"No, that is my interpretation," I said. "So I'm going to ask you a favor. I'm new here, and I've been a teacher for a month, but the one thing they drilled into our heads was that we must never, ever hit a student. When I saw you do that, you compromised me. In the future, don't do that in front of me. You put me in a terrible position."

He didn't speak to me for a long time after that. If I would enter a room, he'd leave. Apparently, I was the asshole. But his students were loyal to him, and I watched from afar to see how he had earned their respect. Was it violence? Was that what it took? No fists, no respect?

Some weeks later, I heard a ruckus outside my classroom, the sound of banging against a metal locker door. I took a look. There was Melvin, handcuffed to a locker, being kneed in the back by a security guard, who was growling, "You want me to lose my job?"

What had he done this time? Melvin was a tough customer, a sociopath with loose wires, born with cocaine in his system to a mother who later died, leaving him to be raised by an elderly grandmother. In class, he was liable to shout out crazy things—anything from sex acts with animals or threats to go home, get a gun and come back and shoot the whole class.

The first time I met Melvin was on a teachers-only day before school started. He was barefoot and shirtless, wearing only shorts, running in short bursts like a commando through the hallways, hiding in doorways. He didn't want to be seen because he wasn't supposed to be inside the school. He came into my classroom to find out who I was and what I was doing there.

"This a Phillips head screwdriver?" he asked me, holding up the tool I'd brought from home. Next time I reached for the screwdriver, it was gone, never to be seen again.

I could only imagine what Melvin had done to get himself hand-cuffed to a locker with a pissed-off security guard's knee in his back.

Seeing me, the guard quit and walked away huffing and puffing. But Melvin was still handcuffed, bringing new meaning to the word "locker." I sent one of my students to fetch Melvin's homeroom teacher, despite second thoughts about calling on someone who had previously cracked the same kid in the head.

To my surprise, that teacher wasted no time advising the necessary parties, in no uncertain terms, that it was against the law to handcuff a student in sight of other students. He demanded that Melvin be uncuffed immediately, and that if the handcuffs had to go back on, he be secured out of sight of other kids.

Students were peering out the windows of doors, stopping in the hallway to listen and watch. They were rapt, silent. This was riveting drama. The teacher did not back down, and it was then that I under-stood why his kids loved him. The kids knew he would crack them when they needed cracking. But they also knew he would defend them when they needed defending.

In their world, that was fair. To them, he represented justice.

In the second month of school, we were halfway through our Marvin Gaye lyric study in eighth-grade language arts when two school secu-rity officers came in with hand-held metal detectors.

There'd been a shooting the afternoon before outside the local high school three blocks away. Two kids were wounded.

We did not have metal detectors at our doors, but security had been on my mind. Before I had assigned lockers, a couple of times shiny, heavy, metal objects clattered onto the wood floor of our classroom. The hair on the back of my neck stood up. Both times, someone dropped a combination lock.

On the day the principal ordered a random check, the students knew what to do. The boys got up and walked slowly to the wall, protesting all the way but smiling and joking. They "assumed the position"—arms up, leaning against the wall, legs spread. They were digging the pat-down, because it made them look bad. But because they were thirteen-year-olds, it was grotesque and heartbreaking.

Gaye wrote in 1971: "Crime is increasing. Trigger-happy policing. Panic is spreading. God knows where it's heading."

I handed out lyric sheets and we listened to two songs, "What's Goin' On" and "Makes Me Wanna Holler." Their homework assignment was to answer one question: What things that Marvin Gaye protested against in 1971 are still problems today? That night, almost everyone did the homework. One girl said while she was working at the kitchen table, her parents picked up her lyrics and burst into song.

"I think Marvin Gaye was saying 'Stop the violence,'" one student wrote. "Nowadays, people are killing for the fun of it."

"Things are still the same—hatred, killing, robberies," another wrote. "I think things are never going to change."

A few more perspectives:

"Marvin Gaye is trying to set things right. He's trying to like send a message to the parents and children to let them do the right thing."

"He said, 'Brothers, there's far too many of you dying' and that's still true because of them pulling out guns to kill each other when they can be friends and work together."

"Marvin Gaye is a good song maker because he makes people feel like they were there."

Some realized they were "there."

"I see lots of stuff 'Going On' and most of it was in the song that we listened to."

"The things Marvin Gaye protested were trigger-happy police and 'panic is spreading.' Just like when they came in with the metal detectors. They searched us because panic was spreading, because two people got shot at _____ High School."

"Marvin Gaye was right. Too many people are dying. I think the boy was wrong, trying to take somebody's life away."

I had tapped into something very real to my students: the sense of peril that pervades their lives each and every day. Danger was a constant threat; they faced a daily struggle for safe passage in the neighborhood.

No wonder the jitters came right through the schoolhouse doors, seeping in like gas, agitating all who breathed it in. It was so very hard to keep violence at bay, so seldom that we were able to make our own peace, to teach and learn in the middle of everything else that was "goin' on."

The same day as our random security check, the cousin of a seventh grader in Astrid's room was killed in a gang shooting.

The shooter who wounded two others outside the high school, meanwhile, was turned in by his mother. He's probably safer in jail, some of my seventh graders observed.

A roving science teacher from the district came once a week to do hands-on projects with the kids.

"You seem to have excellent control of your classroom," he remarked on his first visit. I felt very proud. Four students were at special reading class. The rest sat quietly coloring and assembling their balsa wood airplanes. I sat at my desk and worked on lesson plans. This was nice. This was how I remembered a classroom being when I was in seventh grade. The kids were so good that the guest teacher didn't mind when I left to walk down the hall to drop my plans with my mentor. She had six seventh-grade students from Astrid's class in her office. All were being suspended. I committed the fatal mistake of feeling momentarily superior.

My class is coming around, I told myself.

Twenty minutes later, I was climbing over desks to separate Tyrese and Sherika, who were near the windows, punching each other as the rest of the class crowded around and cheered them on.

A break between rounds.

"Come on. Hit me. Go ahead," Sherika dared in her loud, brash voice.

I stood between them and told them, "Both of you, walk away now. Come on, end this now. That's enough."

Tyrese, who was a full head taller than me, put his hands on my shoulders, gently moved me to the side and proceeded to punch Sherika.

Another girl pulled Sherika back, and Tyrese sort of spun around the room until I browbeat him out the door, but not before another girl started another dustup on his way out about how it was all his fault. Those two got a couple of licks in and continued yelling at each other through the doorway and into the hall.

Their angry voices brought the librarian from across the hall and the special ed teacher from next door. The women hollered at the kids until the security officer came and took all three of the fighters away.

Tyrese's father, who had foster children, adopted children, biological children and grandchildren at the school, often dropped by unannounced. He reminded me of a drill sergeant, and he made a lot of tough decisions when it came to his children, especially his teenagers. I respected him immensely. There he was!

"This isn't the first time you've been in trouble for hitting girls," he berated Tyrese in the hallway. "What are you, some kind of faggot? Is that what it is with you? You have no business putting your hands on this lady, your teacher. You have no business disobeying her or fighting in school. I've had it with you, boy. You belong in boot camp and that's where you're going.

"That's the problem with you boys. Around thirteen, fourteen, you start feeling like you're a man. But you're not a man. It takes a real man to walk away from a fight. It takes a real man not to hit a woman, no matter how mad she makes him."

My mentor, who had already suspended the six other seventh graders, lamented the additional paperwork involved with suspending three more. So I asked Tyrese's father to take him home on an early dismissal instead.

I heard him remark as they walked down the hall, "You are outta control, boy."

The other kids looked somber, exchanged knowing glances. They could only imagine what was in store for Tyrese once his daddy got him home.

The two girls were back in our classroom by lunchtime.

Later, I had the class copy a slogan written by kids their age at an anti-violence camp: "Peacekeepers consider themselves responsible for the integrity of the world, whether their world is the classroom, the school, the community, or the Earth."

"Kids your age wrote that," I told them. "What does it mean to you?"

I asked them, "If you are not a peacekeeper, must I assume you have no integrity?"

Then, I had the students give themselves a grade for behavior that day. They were honest. Destinee, who had led cheers at ringside, gave herself an F-minus. Our final exercise of the day was once again rearranging desks to break up the noisy—and sometimes explosive—partnerships that seemed to form no matter who sat with whom. Made me wanna holler.

Chapter 13

A Five-Week Reorganization

A five-week reorganization brought new levels of angst. I had never heard of such a thing. My children had always had the same teacher from the first day of school to the last. There were no switcheroos unless someone had a baby, got sick, went mental or died.

But apparently a principal has a right to shake things up through the fifth week of school. He can move teachers around and fine-tune the operation if things aren't going well. This, it seems, is an annual event at some schools. It is discretionary and can be used as a reward or a punishment.

That is how Ramona got switched from seventh-grade social studies to a sixth-grade, self-contained classroom and Mr. Diaz joined the seventh- and eighth-grade team. Jennifer, an intern with a third-grade class, got switched to second grade.

At Michelle's school, three fifth grade classes became two. Her twenty-eight students became thirty-six, and her high-achievers went to a veteran teacher. Ramon, an intern who was teaching first grade, was told his position was eliminated. He had a challenging group, but he considered them his, and he was heartbroken. Rather than take another assignment, he dropped out of the program.

Astrid was devastated at leaving her seventh graders and starting over. New faces, new books, new routines. And she had to teach every subject! Her seventh graders gave her a farewell party. They took a collection and raised thirteen dollars. Donna went to Sam's Club and bought a cake decorated with "Movin' On Up!" Astrid's new classroom was on the second floor.

After all the chaos and turmoil of the week, Thursday night's college class was a two-hour group therapy session.

"To wait for this late in the game when they've known all along what's going on is totally unfair," protested Kim.

"This is bullshit," said our normally soft-spoken teacher, who taught first grade for nineteen years and was one of the most gentle people I'd met. "This is not putting kids first. It's jerking you guys around. The thing is, you still have to create a safe, secure place for these kids no matter how you feel."

She suspected that class sizes were purposefully deflated at the start of the year so administrators could tell parents there were twenty-five kids per class. Those low numbers look good on paper. The reality turns out to be quite different.

"How do you make a home when you keep moving?" raged another professor. "This is making it easier for administrators and the budget not you or the kids."

"This is unthinkable anyplace else," said our professor. Anywhere else, "it would not happen."

One intern asked a friend, a vice principal at a North Side school, if this was going on in her part of the city. Her reply, "Where we are, there is no way any of this would be happening."

That intern had to explain to her third graders that they were getting a new teacher. A student asked her, "Why are you giving us up?"

The enormity of the question caused the first-year teacher to lose her composure. She started to cry. Then the kids all started bawling. They spent the rest of the day watching a video. "We couldn't do anything else," she said. "We were wrecked."

"That's what happens with these kids. They've been left with other people, abandoned, forgotten. Then you have them for five weeks, you're starting to bond, then this," said our professor, her face red.

Besides disrupting children's classroom situations, she observed that no one seemed to have given any thought to which children should or shouldn't be together. Most of the kids had been together since they were tiny. They had history together. Yet no teachers seemed to have been asked for insight on the group dynamic. There were cousins with the same surname in the same classroom. At my children's public school, teachers met at the end of the school year to make their lists with an eye toward who worked well with whom and who needed to be separated. At some schools, children spend the last weeks of the school year in their "new" classrooms.

Then again, at a school like mine with a forty percent mobility rate, who knew who would be back?

Year to year, five weeks into the year, changes came.

"Basically what you do is start over," our teacher told us.

Chapter 14

Learning

"**L**ove and respect, people," Donna's voice rang in the corridor. "Love and respect."

That was her mantra, her catch-phrase for interrupting undesirable behavior. That was what she expected of her students and she reminded them of it often.

Down at my end of the hall, Kyisha was sitting in the hallway, her back against the lockers, head down. Tears rolled down her face. She "didn't feel good." Her mother would have kept her home from school, but "had to go to the hospital to visit the twins."

Her mom had given birth a week before to twins. This was the first I'd heard about it. The babies were too tiny to come home yet.

"That makes ten kids," Kyisha said. She and her sister, who was a year older, had the same father.

I handed her a book I checked out of the public library, *Blue Tights*, and let her sit in the overstuffed chair in the book corner. She was soon fast asleep. The chair had become our sick bay and our penalty box, and a prized alternative to the sticky and uncomfortable plastic classroom chairs. With its soft armrests and slanted rolled back, "the big chair" was like a friendly, yielding lap. It was a treat to spread out on the big cushy chair with its swirling upholstery and braided fringe that brushed the floor. It was old and elegant. I bought it at an antique shop years before for about $100. Under the cushion was a velvet panel in a deep teal, a buried treasure. Between its seat and arms, it sometimes held four kids at a time.

Every day I was learning so much about my students and so much from them. In just six weeks I felt so deeply involved in so many lives that the threads wrapped me like a cocoon. I thought of them constantly. I replayed our time together. I talked about them with anyone who would listen. This is what teachers call "reflecting." Pros constantly reflect to troubleshoot and refine their methods and practices. I did it mostly for therapy, as people who survive something cataclysmic keep telling the story until at last they believe it and make a place for it in their psyches.

I found it harder to focus on my own children at home. I had to make a conscious effort to give them my undivided attention when I was with them and not daydream about my other thirty-four children, the ones who perplexed me so. They had changed me.

In six weeks, my students had made me fierce and hard, and it carried over to my own children. Misbehaviors I had once tolerated with a sigh were now shut down without mercy. Still, I tried to be gentle with my students. I gave them chance after chance to break my heart, thinking that maybe that was the only way we could move forward. "Maybe this time we'll succeed" was my constant hope. Finally, it happened.

We had a big project going on that I called "What's in a Name?"

"This week you will complete a research paper about your name. You will use reference books and interview family members to find out:

1. The meaning of your name
2. How your name was chosen for you
3. Whether you were named after someone in particular (a relative, a hero, etc.). If you were named after someone in particular, tell about the person who had your name before you and your connection to this person.
4. Consider the meaning of your name or your 'namesake.' Tell what qualities you draw from either one that you try to exemplify in your life. For instance, if your name means 'brave one,' how do you try to be brave? If you were named after your grandmother, what do you admire about her and try to copy?

5. Were you almost named something else? If so, what was almost your name? How would you feel about having that name instead of the one you were given?
6. Have you ever helped give someone a name? Maybe you helped name a younger sibling or cousin, or a pet! What about giving a nickname to a friend? Tell how you chose the name. Was it easy or difficult?

You must answer all questions. You must attribute all information. That means tell who you talked to and where you got your information.

Wednesday: First drafts due
Thursday: Revisions due
Friday: Present to class
Extra Credit, 5 points each:

• What famous bard asked 'What's in a name?' (Must give author's name and title of play.)
• Bring a baby picture to show the class or a picture of the person you were named after."

Well, no one answered all the questions. Not surprising. It was just too much. But I saw some wonderful baby pictures and learned a lot about African-American names that tongue-tie many white Americans. For instance, a girl might be named "Keitha" by adding the letter "a" to her father's name. A hard decision between "Gwendolyn" and "Brandy" might be solved by inventing the name "Brandalyn." Some names were combinations of parents' names. Some were combinations of mom's best friends' names. Some were traditional African names with significant meaning, like Malik (king) or Imani (faith). Names and naming ceremonies are sacred rites in many cultures.

All that said, when Destinee came to school with an American Girl "Bitty Baby" in her backpack one day, I was astonished that her baby doll had no name. We planned a contest and a naming ceremony to cap our research project.

First, we covered a shoebox with baby wrapping paper and made a slot to cast ballots for name suggestions. We used the baby name book I picked up in the grocery store checkout and two African name books I got at the library. I asked Destinee to choose four "elders" to help her select the name.

The elders, who were actually peers, also copied some lovely sayings from one African book—they were like toasts, full of wisdom and hope—onto index cards. They handed them to other students to read aloud at the ceremony.

Finally, the name was chosen. The class gathered in a circle around Destinee, who presented little "Iglesia Paris Tori Harper-Jones." (Well, not the whole class joined the circle. About six of the usual suspects sat on desks and talked among themselves the whole time. There was some love going on between Kyisha and Tyrese.)

I read out loud from Alex Haley's *Roots*, the part that describes the naming ceremony for Kunta Kinte. Then we passed the baby hand-to-hand, reading the wise sayings from the name book. Freddie was supposed to sing a song but chickened out. Kayla sang something impromptu that sounded like "Lean on Me." DeVille pounded a reggae beat on a desk, and we all joined in. "Lean on Me" turned out to be a perfect song for a naming ceremony.

After our ceremony it was time for library, but I kept a few students with me to "prepare the feast." To prevent a repeat of the 9/9/99 fiasco, I knew I had to be organized, and I'd thought it out step-by-step beforehand.

In *Roots* the villagers ate rice cakes and fruit, so that is what we had. My helpers cut up apples and put blobs of peanut-butter-caramel dip on paper plates at each table, with spoons. There were plenty of napkins. There were no drinks. The helpers were seated at one table, silent and expectant, the perfect dinner guests, when the others came back from library.

"See what they are doing?" I asked, pointing to the models. "Take your seats. Do that."

They did that.

The rice cakes and apples were handed out. We had our snack. The peanut-butter-caramel dip was a huge hit. Some liked it so much they licked it off the spoons and used their fingers to smear it on their rice cakes. Nate went around with the trash can right on schedule. We wiped off the desks with wet paper towels. Only one person had a bathroom emergency, a major issue since a student from 115 swiped my key.

I attributed the success to organization and no drinks. They pleaded to go to the water fountain. They coughed dramatically. No, I demurred, you can make it twelve minutes to the end of school. No one perished from thirst.

It was a good day. It occurred to me that we really ought to sing every day. That was on my mind as I punched out and discovered an exciting development: a memo was posted on the office counter that the superintendent of schools, Paul Vallas, was coming for a visit the next week. He had never visited the school before. There was no specific purpose given for the visit. It was billed as just another of his many visits to neighborhood schools. It set off a flurry of cleaning, decorating and other preparations. A stunning, ceiling-high display case of African-American art was quickly assembled in front of the office.

Meanwhile, the kids had been giving Mr. Diaz the treatment because they were mad about the reorganization. Even though they acted like shit for Astrid, they carried on even worse when she was not their teacher anymore.

The day before the superintendent's visit, my homeroom kids had some sort of riot in social studies. Mr. Diaz called for the assistant principal and our mentor. Next thing I knew, a letter was going home with all seventh graders informing them that they would not be allowed to attend school the next day unless they came with a parent. They were told to come to my room at 9:30.

The superintendent was due at 8:30 and not expected to stay longer than an hour. It was quite brilliant to send the entire seventh grade packing until the coast was clear instead of having them around showboating and making the school look bad.

I doubt it would have bothered Vallas, who pretty much knew the score. I'd known him since he worked as Mayor Daley's finance chief, and you don't survive the back rooms of city hall in Chicago to get shocked by a few seventh-grade punks in a schoolyard. But then again, I did.

The next morning, Vallas spoke to the teachers in the lounge before school. Later, I saw him walk past my room with an entourage. He saw me, too, backed up and came into my classroom, perhaps expecting to find me teaching a riveting lesson in language arts.

Instead, I was facing twenty-six pissed-off parents of twenty-six misbehaving students.

I extended my hand in greeting and welcomed "Mr. Vallas." My students were doubtless surprised to see the CEO kiss me on the cheek and call me "Leslie." I recalled that he had once taught seventh grade, so I told him what was going on and asked him to explain to the students and their caring parents who had come to school that day, why this year was so crucial to their future, why they needed to quit fooling around and get down to business.

He took it from there and delivered an excellent pep talk. I felt certain that the parents took it to heart. They got the main guy, and I got an unexpected boost when Vallas informed them that "Mrs. Baldacci used to be an editor at the *Sun-Times* but came here to teach you because she believes in you." True enough. It was a kick to see him sitting on the table where I sit, talking to my kids. Al Gore's "executive order," still hanging at the front of the room, hadn't done any good. Would they listen to the superintendent of schools?

After Vallas left, the vice principal and the guidance counselor spoke, then Mr. Diaz and myself. I got off my chest some of the careless, dumb stuff that was bugging me. ("Take a look at your child's desk before you leave and in the front of their textbooks. Is your child's name written in white-out inside the desk? In ink on the desk? How many times did he/she write his/her name in the front of the textbook? Enough times so that no one else can ever sign for that book?" As a parent, I asked them not to buy any more school supplies, because they would be sick if they saw how the things they paid money for were destroyed and sicker still if they heard their children refuse to clean up the mess they made, saying "That's the janitor's job.")

The meeting ended with the assistant principal's tirade about junk food and candy and soda pop that the children bring to school (Flamin' Hots and strawberry pop—"Breakfast of Champions") and me in complete agreement, outlining plans for an upcoming research project on healthy eating and fitness.

"Coming soon, to a classroom near you!" I wrapped it up. Everyone laughed. The powwow broke up on a cheerful note. Afterward, parents lingered and I spoke to each one about specific things I was expecting of each child, specific strengths as well as problems each kid needed to work on.

I did not discuss it further with my students. I figured, let them take from it what they would. The message had been clearly delivered: They needed to quit cutting up and engage themselves as learners. The kids fell right back into their bad ways by afternoon, and I made ten phone calls that night.

But I felt we were engaging ourselves as learners on some levels. The most important thing we were learning was how to be readers. I started on the first day of school reading aloud Roald Dahl's *The Witches*, smiling mysteriously but giving no answers to all who asked why I was wearing elbow-length black gloves. "Listen, and you will find out," I told them.

We stopped for the day after the part on page ten that asked, "Which lady is the witch?"

"She might even—and this will make you jump—she might even be your lovely school-teacher who is reading these words to you at this very moment. Look carefully at that teacher. Perhaps she is smiling at the absurdity of such a suggestion. Don't let that put you off. It could be part of her cleverness. I am not, of course, telling you for one second that your teacher actually is a witch. All I am saying is that she might be one. It is most unlikely. But—and here comes the big 'but'—it is not impossible."

I threw back my head and cackled like a witch before removing the gloves, the signal that the read-aloud was over for the day. "Awwwww," they moaned at my cornball tactics.

Not until page twenty-four did they hear the grandmother explain, "A real witch is certain always to be wearing gloves when you meet her...Even in the summer."

"Mrs. B.!" Pierre shouted, pointing. "The gloves!"

Pandemonium.

I learned that there were many fine artists in my classroom, specialists who turned out detailed drawings of cars and action heroes. I asked the class to work on drawings of transformations that occurred in the book, the part in which the boy is turned into a mouse and the part in which the ladies at the convention remove their wigs and masks and are revealed as witches. I thought it would help my visual learners with sequencing.

The captain of the safety patrol, who rarely turned in a speck of work, brought a note in his own handwriting, signed by his church deacon: "Dear Leslie Bodachee. It against my religion to draw evolution, including witchcraft or any other evolution."

The thought had never entered my head that witchcraft, even in a fictional children's story, and especially evolution, would offend some fundamentalist Christians. I had been insensitive. It made me wonder about Halloween and fairy tales and *Harry Potter*. In the future I'd better ask first, I realized, and have another option for those with religious objections. That deacon must have wondered what on earth these children were learning in that classroom with a heathen for a teacher.

"Find something to read independently while we work on our novel," I told the student. When we finished the book, the class watched the movie, and enjoyed it very much. I offered to let the religious protester go to another classroom, but he declined. He seemed to enjoy the movie and even participated in our "compare and contrast" exercise on the book vs. movie version, which was rich and detailed. Those kids didn't miss a trick.

Our second novel was *Maniac Magee* by Jerry Spinelli. It seemed to have a hypnotizing effect on certain surprising individuals: Eric, Freddie, Nichelle, and Destinee. Eric's mouth finally quieted, and I caught Freddie sitting, slack-jawed, looking into space, as I was reading. I could practically see the movie show rolling in his brain. He was somewhere else, and I know exactly where that was because he remembered every fact of the story when we summarized out loud. Every fact.

The kids complained at first about being read to every day, but when they saw I was not going to stop, they sat back and enjoyed it. Children need to be read to. Big kids think it's babyish, but it's not. It is an act of love and it creates connections. It is helpful to have a story "modeled" by a good reader. It hones listening skills. I made up daily quizzes and asked open-ended questions that they had to think about and answer on paper. *Maniac Magee* gave us much to think about in terms of how Americans divide themselves along color lines and how little some of us know and how much we assume about people whose skin color is different from our own.

The school had a day when we could dress up as characters from books. I wore a baseball cap and jeans and cut the soles of an old pair of sneakers so that they slapped the ground when I walked. My students knew in an instant that I was Maniac Magee. But outside the classroom, the principal told me to remove the hat. It was against the dress code. He was unmoved by my protest that I was in character and celebrating a book that was important to my class.

We read three more novels as read-alouds. Through the public library, I gathered enough copies of the book *Shiloh* for everyone to read along with a partner while I played a books-on-tape version on our boom box. Strangely, that was the novel that bombed, either for lack of interest or the break in our routine. Maybe they missed me reading to them. Maybe that part of our day had become special to them.

I learned that they were ignorant of geography. They didn't know the states; they had vague ideas of continents. I decided to craft a research project around travel so they'd get some geography along with language arts.

The project was planning their dream trip. I went to a couple of travel agents and grabbed every glossy brochure I could get my hands on.

They had to decide where they wanted to go and how far it was from Chicago. They had to determine the cost, pack a suitcase and write an itinerary of sight-seeing and other activities specific to their destination. They had to find out the currency, language, what different foods they might eat and what were good souvenirs to buy. They had to convert currency and account for time zones.

Destinations included Mexico, Jamaica, Africa, Wyoming, Florida, California and England. Andre wanted to go to Paris, of course. Good thing we were still working on our French. We had learned numbers, colors, clothing, phrases and an innocuous swear word or two. "*Zut alors!*" We worked it in when we could. "*Bonjour, classe,*" I would often start the day. "*Bonjour, madame,*" they'd reply with gusto. In Social Studies, it helped to know French when we learned who settled New Orleans and Baton Rouge ("Red Stick"). When we were studying the weather in science, we'd ask, "*Quel temps fait-il?*" and learned the words for snow and rain and cold and hot. When we wrote letters to Fred Montgomery, curator of the Alex Haley Museum, Andre started his letter, "Bonjour, Mr. Montgomery," which made me smile. We learned some Spanish, too.

The dream trip project, with its cross-curricular integrations of math and social studies, came in handy when, two days before first-quarter report card pick-up, our principal informed Mr. Diaz and me that our worst fear had been realized: the upper grades would no longer be departmentalized. No more changing classes. Each of us would teach all subjects to our homerooms. Starting that day.

Apparently, he had decided this some weeks before. He had informed the eighth-grade teachers the week before. "I should have told you, too. My fault. Apologies," he said curtly before turning on his heel and walking away.

We were in shock. Suddenly, we were on the hook for lesson plans in all subjects, coming up to speed on the curriculum and teaching the lessons. But that was only a week-by-week crisis. The deeper crisis was whether we were up to the task of teaching our students in all subjects. Seventh-grade standardized test scores determine a child's high school options. What if my ineptitude kept someone from getting into an accelerated program or a better high school? I'd become comfortable with language arts. This new responsibility was daunting.

Donna, who had been a teacher for twenty-six years, was so upset and frustrated at the order that she cussed out the vice principal and walked out. She lined up job interviews at other schools. She tried to console me.

"This is only your first year," she reminded me. "If I can't handle it after all these years, of course you're gonna be overwhelmed. It's only natural. But God wouldn't give you anything you can't handle, you know that. You'll get through this."

If she left, I would be so sad. She was my rock, and I told her so. I felt like I imagined a rock felt, like *Sylvester and the Magic Pebble*. I was numb.

Somehow I dragged myself to a party downtown, even though it was four days before payday and I was broke. I drove around until I found a meter, then walked. After two months in flats, high heels were agony. But dipping back into my old life for an evening, the shoes fit and I felt like Cinderella. It was great to see everyone. I showed around our class picture, which I had received that day. I thought it was a really nice picture, but one former colleague said it made him want to cry. I shared a piece of fiction writing titled *Pimps Up, Hypes Down* with Mary. We howled at the depth of lowbrow reached in this particular group-writing exercise. Three boys recounted, with gross misspelling and punctuation errors, their future achievements: They earn tons of money "selling weed" and shoot people in the butt who cross them. In the end, they become "successful rapers." We're pretty sure they meant "rappers." On one hand, it made us want to cry. But we had the good sense to laugh instead.

"You have your work cut out for you," Mary observed.

Kayla reminded me of Mary, who grew up in public housing on the South Side and whose salvation was the Chicago Public Library Book-mobile. I was floored after our first round-robin when Kayla delivered a splendid read-aloud to rival any radio anchorwoman.

Later that week, she expressed an interest in reading Nancy Farmer's *A Girl Named Disaster*. I had it waiting for her on her desk the next morning. The following day she arrived on the playground with her face in the book, halfway through. She had read about 150 pages. "Up late last night?" I asked. She nodded.

I let her stay in that book all day. I didn't bother her. If she was reading, as far as I was concerned, she was participating at the highest possible level.

As the group left the building that day, she lifted her face from the book, broke out of line and ran to me, giving me a hug and a kiss on the cheek before flitting out the door. She would be done with the book tomorrow, I realized. What should I give her next? Hmmm. Something fatter.

That year she read *A Tree Grows in Brooklyn*, *To Kill a Mockingbird*, all the *Harry Potter*s, three Sharon Creech novels, some F. Scott Fitzgerald and at least a dozen other books. Each received the same review: "This was the best book I have ever read."

Kayla was also a good reader of emotions. She always seemed to know when I needed a boost. She always had a hug after a particularly grisly day. It wasn't until after she was gone that I would figure out how a child could read adult emotions so clearly and be so generous in sharing her strength and support. I came to depend on her—to know the answers in class, to turn in homework, to offer suggestions on how we could do things better in our class.

She was used to having adults depend on her. I would not learn why until spring.

Chapter 15

An Observation

When my graduate school advisor came to observe, she was so upset that she called for the mentor and the principal.

"This is a joke," she informed them. The kids were mad about not changing classes any more. They were acting up.

"Thirty-six middle-class, self-disciplined, academically gifted kids in one class is a joke. These undisciplined children, crammed together with assorted behavior problems, is an unteachable situation."

The principal explained that there were two seventh-grade classrooms and nowhere else to put the kids. He told her the kids were the problem.

"They didn't get this way since September," she noted. Just then, to prove her point, a lower grade classroom ran past, screaming.

She reminded the mentor that her job was to spend an hour each day in each intern's room, co-teaching and modeling for us how to teach.

The mentor replied that she was the "disciplinarian."

"You're the mentor," my advisor told her. "If you can't do that job, maybe someone else should. And maybe if this school can't give these interns the support they need, Teachers For Chicago doesn't belong in this school."

I prayed they wouldn't pull us out. In my opinion, this was precisely the sort of school that desperately needed scrutiny, and Teachers For Chicago was the foot in the door that might provide a crack of that light. I decided I couldn't bear to leave. There were so many things I had learned already but much I needed to find out.

Why didn't any parents know about magnet schools they could apply to so their kids didn't have to go to school here? Why weren't there any television sets or VCRs? The librarian said they were all stolen. Why hadn't insurance paid to replace the stolen equipment? Why were there so few books in the library? Why was it dark and empty so many hours? Why didn't the upper grades get time in the computer lab? Were chronic, truly dangerous kids ever sent to alternative schools? Every warm body that brought in cold cash, it seemed, was allowed to stay. The bottom line was, I couldn't leave the class. The upset of the reorganization made me realize how desperately they needed continuity. There had to be some value in coming back day after day, trying hard, doing my best, even if my best was woefully inadequate. Those were the only terms under which I could ask the same from them.

After the advisor left, the principal and mentor returned to my room.

"Where's your fire escape plan?" asked my mentor.

"Hanging right there, by the door," I said, pointing to the pink sheets. The children watched, rapt.

"Where's your schedule?"

"Nichelle, please put up the map at the back of the room. The schedule is behind it."

"Where's your grading scale?"

"Bulletin board, lower right corner."

"Where's your time distribution chart?"

"I don't know what that is."

"You should have it posted in the classroom," she said. "Have it on my desk at eight o'clock tomorrow morning."

They turned and left. It was the second-oldest trick in the book—when someone makes trouble for you, nickle and dime them to death on paperwork that has nothing to do with either teaching or learning.

I was more confused than ever the next morning when my mentor came into my classroom, fuming about how she'd been told to spend more time in our classrooms, before turning on her heel and walking out.

I was confused because the people who were supposed to support me and teach me were treating me like an enemy. They wanted a seating chart. And children's names in books and books numbered. All of which I certainly should have done, if I'd only known.

In the teachers' lounge I said hello to a substitute. He said he taught at our school for four years before quitting at the end of last year.

"Why?" I asked.

"Can't build a house with no tools," he said simply.

Chapter 16

Crime and Punishment

Kyisha and a girl across the hall had been at war all week. I picked up on the vibe and watched them like a hawk. In the morning, I separated them before they came to blows. The principal was in the hallway and took them to the office. By the time I had their "office referral" forms written up, they were back in their classrooms, claiming that they had put their differences aside.

But at dismissal, the whole class burst from the room and ran out of the building like a herd of deranged wildebeests. I followed them outside. Something was up. I saw Kyisha standing on the steps with her coat off in the November chill, looking dangerous, breathing heavily.

I steered her aside. "Where are you going?" I asked.

"Home," she said. I walked her off the steps and a little way, pointed her toward her house and told her to keep going.

As I walked back inside the building, the other girl came running down the hall from the far door, claiming that Kyisha had tried to beat her up with a weapon made from a bicycle chain with two combination locks hooked to one end. I sat her in the office and went looking for Kyisha.

The dangerous vapors of violence lingered in the air. The mood carried over.

Pierre, who was attracted to violence as flies to Kool-Aid, picked up the battle cry and had a rock 'em, sock 'em dust-up with a student from across the hall as the kids came in the next morning. The brother of the other student dove into the fray, and furniture was knocked around. I managed to pluck the smallest one from the tangle when he came up for air. I carried him on my hip out into the hallway. A crowd had gathered, hooting and jeering.

A fight could set the tone for the whole day. The kids were off-task, completely juiced up. They wouldn't come back to class from the lunchroom. They couldn't settle down to work on their fiction writing. They couldn't organize themselves into groups of four. My mentor, frosty since the observation, had been missing in action for two days. I screamed so much that day my throat was sore.

By day's end, one fighter was contrite, but Pierre was acting like a wronged innocent. Each got five days, same as Kyisha.

The following Monday, four more of my boys got suspended for another episode, so our class was under thirty students.

DeVille, one of the suspended, left shouting a warning over his shoulder that his mother would be at school first thing in the morning "to get me back in." He had gotten in trouble for throwing food in the lunchroom and shooting beans with a rubber band in the classroom. Though I had seen him do both things with my own eyes, he denied everything. He also claimed he didn't break our stapler, but I found the spring in his desk.

With so many key troublemakers gone, everything changed. It was as if a fog lifted and the sun came out. We finished all of our lessons. We were orderly. We had several discussions, one about what they would do if they were followed by a stranger and another about whether fear is a choice or an instinct. Eric participated for the first time that year. He told three stories and later ordered Tyrese to "quit fooling around." Tyrese was at looser ends than usual without his buddies to clown with. At one point, he sat next to me on the big table, because he simply didn't know what else to do with himself, and it was the only place he could still feel like he was in charge, now that his power base had been eliminated. He was my co-teacher.

I had been keeping records on the number of times he disrupted class. According to my log, on a typical morning, in a two-hour period, he would leave his seat fifteen times, shout out about two dozen times and display "oppositional behavior" about five times.

At the end of the day, I asked the class to respond in writing to the question, "Does today feel different than other days in 118? How?"

Here's what they said:

"Straight because most of the talkers are gone. It was peaceful and quiet today. Okay."

"Things have gotten a little quieter than usual and there is less chaos."

"Today with 27 students is different because the students that talk too much are not here. It's not loud like it use to be when they are here."

"It is going along good and fast with only 30 students. Well my day did."

"Today the class was quiet. I think the teacher got away almost all the troublemakers in I think it's better like this."

"I think that we did more work today than any other day."

"GREAT. And we can get even more work done if you want us to cause everyone cooperated today."

"Yes because it is so quiet and aint no body running around the room."

"It was different because, on most days we don't get most of our lesson done but, today we got our work done. Because the troublemakers isn't here to mess up our day and usually the troublemakers have our teacher stressed out, but, she doesn't seem stressed out today."

Kayla, the voracious reader, wrote, "How is today different from most days in 118? Well, it's different because when there here its a mess papers are everywhere it just horrible that why I think today is a grand happy exciting lovely optimistic magical day." All that reading was having an impact on her vocabulary, if not her punctuation.

"It is very different today without most of the bad kids but today is a nice day no hollering, cursing, fighting today is a great day. Without those bad kids in here starting stuff."

"Our class wasn't to loud, we wasn't getting in trouble as much as we always do and there was nobody interrupting our class like almost everyday. And the class didn't get in trouble because of someone else."

"Today is more quiet and peaceful and I like it. I wish we always have a smaller group."

I talked to every single student that day. I spent time with children who did excellent work, my hardcore learners whom I never had a chance to really "be" with because I was so busy quelling the misbehavers. The kids who had endured nine weeks of that nonsense were still with me, and we reached a critical mass. It truly was a wonderful day. We saw each other at our best.

I wrote a memo to the principal thanking him for his support and sharing with him the students' comments. I gave it to him the next morning. At 12:30, I was summoned for a "review meeting."

I asked Donna what this meant. She advised me to "go in with the full armor of God," along with my grade book and attendance book.

In the meeting, the principal expressed his displeasure that I did not correct the children's comments into standard English for my memo. Then he gave me an article that appeared on the *Tribune* op-ed page about how the teachers' union protects the inept.

He asked me for my impressions of the year so far and to give a self-assessment of my work. I asked whether there were any particular points he would like me to address, any specific areas. He said no. So I told him it had been the most challenging nine weeks of my professional life, that no one could have prepared me for what I face every day. I told him that I found it thrilling, compelling, even despite the hardships, and that I never once regretted my decision. I waited for him to respond.

He spoke of the suspended students. "These children are victims." He said we must conduct ourselves with love, kindness and understanding. He said that when students were suspended they were unsupervised and that concerned him. He said they needed to be in school not out of school.

He hinted that he would give me some feedback as to what he thought of my professional performance so far. But we were interrupted when a student's mother came in to complain about a teacher slapping her son, and our meeting was over, to be continued later in the afternoon. It never was, and that was my only "review" until the horrible surprise meeting at the end of the year, when all of my misdeeds and shortcomings were thrown in my face.

But I did listen to what the principal told me, and the next day, when Pierre had a tantrum and sulked all day because I had someone else do the attendance, I tried to behave differently, kinder.

I took him out in the hallway and asked him what he was so all-fired mad about. He confirmed that it was because he wanted to take care of the attendance.

"But I have to train others so that if you're not here, someone else knows how to do it. You have to share what you know. Do you really think it's worth ruining a whole day over?"

"No," he said, still mad.

"You know I love you and you are the best assistant any teacher could ever want," I said.

"All right," he said, looking at his feet and trying to suppress a smile.

Things went better after that.

Chapter 17

Thanksgiving Break

Thanksgiving, my favorite holiday. Bliss. The girls and I went to Baltimore for a three-day house party at my parents'. In the warm embrace of my tribe, I found sustenance among my family's many career educators.

My brother and his wife and two kids came up from Norfolk, my sister and her two kids were there. My cousins came with their children. The cousins frolicked, we wore ourselves out talking and cooking.

Both my cousins' parents and mine were career educators. My father was the athletic director at my cousins' high school; my uncle was athletic director at mine. His wife was an elementary principal and my mother taught high school and college. Her sister, my Aunt Joan, worked at a tough high school in Pittsburgh, where she was known as "the motherfucking nurse."

I thought I was the only second-generation teacher in the bunch, which is unusual. In many families, teaching is a craft passed on from generation to generation. Some families are education Mafias. My parents, on the other hand, thought I was crazy to become a teacher, especially in the setting and era I chose. But they had been highly supportive, clipping newspaper articles, sending boxes of books and giving me money to buy supplies for my classroom. They phoned me every weekend for debriefings and advice.

"How's Kayla?" my mother would ask. "What's Tyrese up to?"

Over the Thanksgiving break, I learned that my sister-in-law taught math for two years fresh out of college at an alternative school for behavior-disordered kids in the South. Wow. I'd known her for fifteen years and never knew she was once a teacher. (One-third of new teachers drop out by the third year; she left because her family moved to another state.) Her experience sounded strangely similar to my own.

"I thought I was a terrible teacher," she said. "I felt completely incompetent, that it was criminal that I was responsible for those children."

She gave me a great bit of advice—connect with the kids on an emotional level. Be real with them. Her kids voted her "Teacher of the Year" the month before she left.

My cousin's wife taught special education for eight years. They later adopted three daughters, two with special needs. She was home schooling them.

I'd always thought of Mary as unflappable. She was unfailingly calm and jolly. Yet she admitted she thought she'd lost her mind as a first-year teacher.

"I thought I was having a nervous breakdown," she said. "I had no idea what I was doing, there was no one to help me, I was copying things weekends and evenings for curriculum. I had hives all the time!"

"Me, too," chimed in Bernadette, my sister-in-law. "I kept cortisone cream in my top drawer."

Try to imagine a job so stressful it gives you hives. But neither one quit over hives. That perspective was far more helpful than the corporate analogy that policymakers drag out when they say schools should run like efficient businesses, with teachers the CEOs of their own small corporations. The teacher/CEO runs all departments: the business office, stocking all supplies and materials; human resources for the "employees'" assorted personal needs (especially the team-building issues that far exceed the demands of adults in a professional situation); quality assurance through assessment and retraining. Above all, the CEO/teacher must be accountable.

In a teacher's corporation, however, the CEO does not hire the employees and cannot fire them. Many come in inept, unreliable and combative. The teacher has nine months to turn the crew into a smooth-running organization. Then they all quit. The next year, the teacher starts over with thirty-five new employees who are inept, unreliable and combative...

It was a tonic to be in the warm embrace of my sympathetic and supportive family. I came home to Chicago and slept for three hours. On Sunday I went to church and graded papers in bed. Monday I felt great. I got up ready to do battle. My optimism bubbled up once again.

Chapter 18

An Intervention

DeVille was out of control, so during library one Friday I kept Nate, Kayla and two other responsible souls who comprised my new Peer Intervention Team in the classroom.

DeVille was our subject. The others were to tell him, kindly but firmly, what about his behavior was bothering them personally and the impact it was having on our class. I asked them to begin by reminding him—and themselves—that they were friends and cared about him. We sat around the big table. It was quiet and sunny.

Racquel started: "DeVille, we've been friends a long time, since pre-school, but it's time for you to grow up. You clown around too much. You talk too much. We are here to learn and you are dragging us down..."

Kayla evangalized: "It's time to quit fooling around DeVille and decide what kind of man do you want to be."

Nate: "DeVille, man, we've been knowing each other a long time now, and it's time to quit acting all crazy in school..."

DeVille was silent. Then he said, "I don't have to listen to this." He got up and walked out of the room. I went after him and quietly implored him to come back. I explained it was now time for him to respond and that we weren't leaving the table without a contract, a promise from him that he would mend his ways and get on board.

He flounced into his seat. "You can sit here all day. I'm not going to make a promise I can't keep," he said.

"What makes you think you can't keep a promise, DeVille?" I asked.

"I don't make promises," he said.

"It's scary to make promises," I told him. "But it's time you took responsibility for yourself and commit yourself. We all believe in you or we wouldn't be here."

Stonewall. Silence. Arms folded. Looking out the window. It was still and golden in the slanting afternoon sun. A lull fell over us. We were waiting. Donna called this "God's silence," the time after you express a need honestly and wait for something to happen. Sometimes it's a long wait.

I asked, "DeVille, did someone break a promise to you? Is that why you won't take the chance of making your own promise?"

His face crumpled. Huge hot tears sprang from his eyes and rolled down his face. "It's my daddy," he said, sobbing. "He promised me he'd always be there for me."

I felt like I'd been kicked in the chest.

Again, he walked out of the room. Again, I went after him. I waited. We stood there. I handed him a tissue. He wiped his eyes.

"You all are ganging up on me," he said. "It's not fair. I'm not going back in there."

"DeVille, you heard everyone in there. The first thing each one said was 'You are my friend.' They all care about you. I care about you. We see your behavior dragging you down. You need to decide what you stand for not your daddy. We wouldn't be here if we didn't believe you could make that stand. Now wipe off your face, take a few deep breaths and give me your hand."

He wiped his eyes. Reluctantly, he trudged back in.

I wrote out the promise. He sat with his arms folded and refused to sign. We sat a while in silence.

"DeVille," I finally asked him, "is there something I do that really bugs you, something I could promise not to do any more?"

"Well," he said, "it really bugs me when you scream 'DeVille!' every time something goes wrong in the classroom."

"Ouch," I said. "Yeah, I can see how that would get old. It's not fair, and it's something I should work on. If I sign a promise to you not to scream 'DeVille!' will you sign your part of the deal?"

Another long silence. He looked down at the table. Finally, a nod.

I signed a document that said "I promise not to scream 'DeVille!' any more." I added my middle name to my signature and his mouth twitched the tiniest bit with amusement. He signed his part of the deal—a promise not to talk, walk around the room, goof off in the hallways, disrupt the class. We put the two halves in his pant-leg pocket.

"You keep it there to remind you of your promise," I said. "All of you can remind me of mine if I mess up. I might mess up, but I'm going to try my best to keep my promise. Our business is finished for now. Everyone shake hands."

Some were doing better than others about resolving conflict.

Kyisha and Kayla had a dust-up before school one morning that caused Kayla to arrive sobbing. She sat with her face buried in her arms on her desk for the first hour of school.

Later, I heard that Kyisha had told her she was "so ugly (she) couldn't get a date with a roach."

I pulled Kyisha aside after lunch and asked her about it. She confirmed she had said that, but said Kayla "started it."

"She said she was too smart to be with such a bunch of losers."

"You were both wrong," I said. "Why don't you be the peacemaker and be the first to set things right?"

I told her I expected a written apology before the close of business that day. Kyisha passed me an envelope late in the afternoon. It was an exchange between the two:

"Kayla, I'm sorry for saying that mean statement to you. But you owe us (everyone) in this class an apology also because you shouldn't said what you said about your to good because everyone is equal but I am sorry and I expect to hear from you.

Deepest compassion,

Kyisha"

Kayla responded, "Well I am sorry for what I said, but see they like to say un-nice things. I forgive them and especially forgive you Kyisha."

I was proud of the way the girls handled their business.

But my heart ached for the boy who missed his daddy. I understood the secret sadness that his clowning hid. He was one of many millions of children who live every day with a father's absence fraying the edges of their lives. They worry about their fathers and if they're all right. They wonder what it is about them that makes them unworthy of a phone call or a visit. They wonder what is it about them that made their father go away and never come back. They see it not as the profound failure of an adult but as a personal failing of their own. They start believing that they weren't good enough or their daddy would surely come see them, see how they're doing, see how they're growing up, see how they're doing in school.

Chapter 19

The Bathroom Incident

As the winter days grew short, I found that going back to school put me back in touch with the seasons of childhood, when emotions and routines are keenly connected to the seasons of nature. Four seasons, four report cards. Forty weeks in a school year, nearly the same amount of time it takes to create human life.

Fall crackled with leaves underfoot and the excitement of new beginnings, new challenges, new school supplies, new clothes. Because I was born on Labor Day, I probably clock the start of the school year as the beginning of a cycle more keenly than most people. Some years my birthday falls on the holiday; some years it's the first day of school. I prefer the holiday.

As fall deepened, the swirling leaves outside our classroom windows reflected the whirlwind of activity inside. The Thanksgiving break and a change of scene, plus the support and wisdom of my extended family, reminded me of the need for connections. The first flurries reminded me that I must make our classroom a haven—not just from the bite of winter but from the bite of the outside world. We had so many forces pulling us apart, would we ever become a unified team? Why had it been so hard for me to take charge of my class, the shortcoming for which I was criticized time and again?

"Your lesson plans are dynamite, but they don't mean anything if you can't control your class," my mentor told me many times. According to her, she had been a master teacher whose students obeyed her every command and performed beyond all expectations. I believed her because she was a commanding presence. She could "talk the walk," as she had once said. However, I had yet to see her in action. She never

taught a lesson in my classroom. Her help was limited to crowd control and troop movement, for which I was grateful. A couple of times,
she supplied materials from the bookshelves that lined the walls of her
office. On occasion, she took small groups of my students to her office.

"What do you do there?" I'd ask them.

Talk, do worksheets, help file things, run errands around the school,
straighten bookshelves, they told me. I was grateful that her door was
open to the students, because it gave me some relief, especially during
our long afternoons. That same door was often not open to me, however, especially since the criticism from my college advisor. During the
day, the door was often shut and locked. The window had been covered with construction paper, so it was impossible to tell whether anyone was in there. It reminded me of an editor I once worked for who
worked behind closed doors while listening to music on headphones.
We'd flap our arms from the other side of the glass partitions in dead-
line emergencies. Our mentor left at 2:30 sharp every afternoon, while
we were dismissing our students, so we had no opportunity to meet
with her after school.

I was grateful for whatever bone she threw me, though, especially
helping with bathroom breaks. I was terrible at bathroom breaks. It
seemed I never could accomplish one without an incident. What was
so hard about unlocking the bathroom doors, monitoring eighteen boys
in one bathroom and eighteen girls in another, getting them all back in
line, then relocking the doors? (I'd like to see the chairman of General
Motors give it a try.)

The bathrooms were located at a stairwell, at the intersection of the
main hallway and a short hallway with two sets of doors to the outside.
There was always some sort of mischief. The girls would sprawl on the
steps, talking louder and louder, their voices carrying up the stairwell to
the upstairs hallway. Someone feeling frisky might open a door to the
outside and take a peek, poised to bolt. The boys roughhoused relent-
lessly in the privacy of their bathroom, peeing on one another, shooting
water from the sink faucets, making toilets overflow, scrawling graffiti
on the walls. Fights broke out in there. Tyrese once slammed a kid's
head into a pipe and gave him a gash that required stitches.

There were so many things I needed to be on top of, and time after time I failed. One part of me realized that bathroom breaks have nothing to do with teaching or learning, but I became consumed with the importance of order in the hallways because that is the only time anyone saw my class. No one ever came to observe. Or so I thought.

My harping about the broken chalkboard of death behind the AV screen finally brought the principal to my room, when I complained again after a staff meeting in the library before school. He walked across the hall to take a look. The liability must have been apparent, because he immediately summoned both janitors. They removed the most dangerous hunks of slate and produced a cork bulletin board to cover the hole and remaining slate. With the principal holding up the cork board and the janitors drilling it in place, our class worked on an assignment amid the din of hammering and drilling. Later, at a meeting during which I was threatened with firing, the principal would resurrect that vignette as evidence that I did not observe the posted time for reading instruction. Another failing he cited was that I allowed students to go to the bathroom in pairs without supervision, which I found necessary as more of my girls began menstruating and needed greater access to the bathroom.

Funny how the girls' bathroom was the setting for an incident that marked a turning point for us. That was where I learned an important lesson that didn't come out of any book.

Kyisha had gotten into a loud, profane fight with Tyrese and another boy who had been talking trash about her. She and Tyrese had been "going out" for a while. Then they weren't. Then this happened. She was threatened with a twenty-day suspension for "starting it."

After school, I found about eight of my girls in the bathroom, where Kyisha was sobbing.

"It's not fair," she wailed. In the high-blown emotion of a teenage girl with her own sharp mind, she saw a ladder of injustice. Why was she getting suspended from school when the grownups in charge were getting away with not doing their jobs?

"How can he say he's gonna suspend me for twenty days when he's not doing his job?" she implored. "We got no books, people steal everything out of your desk and people who get sent out come right back in.

Look, our bathrooms got no doors. People wreck everything. And the boys are all up there saying all this mean stuff. It's not fair. It's like everyone's against us."

We looked around us at the bathroom. No doors on the stalls, no mirrors, two stopped-up sinks and peeling paint. Everything around us seemed to prove her point. I thought of my overstuffed chair. A couple of days before, someone had smeared black ink all over the seat cushion and the armrests. I thought of the abandonment I felt as I struggled to be the teacher of these children.

She was right. It wasn't fair. Tears filled my eyes, too, and spilled down my cheeks. We all started to cry.

"You have every right to feel that way," I told her, my voice breaking. "It's not fair that we don't have supplies and that people wreck everything. I feel that way, too, sometimes, with our class."

We stood and sniffed in silence a while. I swore I would never cry in front of my students, no matter how bad it got, just as I've never cried in front of a boss when things broke bad. Now I had done that. Even though it was in a broken-down bathroom after school hours, by the next day everyone would know I had cried. I had given up any pretense of control.

"Girls, we have to pull ourselves together," I said, wiping my face off. "We can't let ourselves get dragged down to someone else's low level. We have to keep going, even when things aren't fair, even when everything seems to be against us. There is no other choice. We have to keep our heads up. We have to go forth with as much dignity as we possibly can and without violence."

They were still crying, but they were listening.

It isn't going to get any easier, I told them. You girls are smart and sensitive enough to recognize injustice, so you, more than anybody, can't give up. People who see these things are the ones who have to change them. That is our responsibility as thinking women. We have to keep going.

Come on, I said. Let's go.

We hugged. We wiped our faces. We mustered our dignity. We went forth.

The pact we made that day is probably what kept me from walking out the schoolhouse door on any given day. Children learn by example, and so did I. As long as they kept coming back, so would I.

There were no repercussions to my tearful breakdown. Control, I realized, was overrated. Likewise, staying out of trouble. You can have control and stay out of trouble and still not be a good teacher.

I took heart in the example of my college math teacher, Alonza Everage, who taught me more about understanding and appreciating numbers than I'd ever thought possible.

"I was in trouble the whole time I was a teacher," he said. One of the things he got in trouble for was holding class in a beautiful plant-filled atrium at his school. The principal told him, "Students aren't allowed in this area."

He was back the next day, teaching in the atrium.

Our college professors turned out to be the role models our mentors often were not. I was not the only intern whose reinforcements were no-shows, not the only one whose mentor was used as an extra administrative assistant to the principal. Some interns had it worse. Their mentors were cronies of the principal and treated the year like a sabbatical. They were completely missing in action, attending workshops that had nothing to do with the program, hiding in the computer lab sending e-mails to their friends and making fliers for their outside businesses. None of them ever got in trouble.

Chapter 20

A Winning Streak

The day before the science fair, the tri-fold display boards were not much to look at. After years of annual science fair projects with my own children, I recognized a lack of parent involvement rather than a lack of student effort. To complete a project and put a board together requires parent backup. It doesn't happen on its own. Kids need parents to take them to the library and shopping for materials and art supplies. Parents first must be aware of the timetable, then police it. They need to make time for kids to get together to conduct experiments and put together the board. They need to help kids compile and analyze the data, to question and help kids make sense and organize their findings. As a parent, I dreaded the science fair every year. It was like being a teacher for the weekend. How ironic to find myself in a classroom surrounded by dozens of problematic science fair projects.

Donna and the special science teacher had taken the kids as far as they could. Donna even had boards for sale, with printed labels: hypothesis, data, conclusion and all that jazz. But what came dragging in the day before the fair was pretty raggedy for the most part. It was utterly predictable who had the good experiments and boards. All were children with involved parents: Carlos, whose mother monitored him closely and came up for conferences, the new girl whose parents took her places on weekends, and a girl whose mother was looking into other schools for her smart, spunky daughter.

"All right, you rocket scientists, here's what we're gonna do. We're gonna help each other the best we can," I informed the fidgety masses. I had them look at each other's boards and suggest improvements. We hauled out all of our glue, construction paper, crayons and rulers and spent the day helping each other with organization, charting data and sprucing up the boards. Now I was grateful for all those dreaded science projects over the years.

The fair took place on Tuesday in the gym. Everyone dressed to the nines. Some looked like they were going to church, others to a dance. There were three-piece suits and strappy dresses with heels. The excitement of dressing up, getting sprung from class for the day and the schedule change was thrilling. All morning long, they explained their projects for the judges and class after class of little kids.

Unfortunately, when lunchtime finally came, there was a stampede from the gym. The assistant principal decided that was all the science fair the seventh grade could handle. It did not resume after lunch.

The winners were Nelson, with his box guitar; Carlos and a partner for their rocket balloon; and the two girls with the involved parents, who took first place with their "layers of liquid" experiment.

The class rallied around our winners and took pride in sweeping the competition. They ridiculed the other seventh-grade class, yelling across the hall "118 rules! 115 sucks!" I dragged them back inside for a talking-to on the importance of being gracious winners, lest we become losers in the process of winning.

We'd had so few opportunities to be winners. We were virtually on lockdown due to behavior problems. No field trips were allowed. No computer lab. Many days at gym they sat on the floor while the teacher waited for them to quiet down, and when that didn't happen, they never even stood up. The one teacher to take them outside was the traveling science teacher, to fly their balsa-wood planes.

The science fair victory lifted expectations for the upcoming Christmas pageant. The kids were dying to perform. Pierre, who was active in his church and had the voice of an angel, stepped up as our choir director. (We had a wonderful art teacher but no music at school.) I asked Pierre to please take one verse for a solo, but he declined.

"Mrs. B., I'm happy right here where I am," he said.

"All right then, Pierre, stay there," I told him. I gave him the official title of "artistic director of 118." To this day, when I watch the video of their performance, I marvel at Pierre's professionalism. There was not a cross word between him and any other student the whole time they worked on the Christmas program. It must have been a Christmas truce. Usually the other students, especially the boys, antagonized Pierre all the time, calling him "gay" and inciting him to high drama and violence for their own amusement.

The children chose their own music: a medley of Kirk Franklin's "Melody from Heaven" and "Joy to the World." I had an idea, too, that DeVille and I worked out before we showed it to the class. First I read the beginning of *The Night Before Christmas* in standard English. But after a few verses I asked DeVille to "give me a beat" and I started over, rapping the same parts. By the time I got to "not a creature was stirring, not even a mouse," the kids were clapping along. They were excited about it and wanted to do the whole poem as a rap. DeVille and Joseph volunteered to be our drummers. They played the big table with their hands.

We copied the entire poem by hand, then divided up the verses. Pierre and DeVille figured out a way to segue the beat from the song to the rap, and Racquel's posse put the heat on everyone to get a Santa cap at the Dollar Store.

In just a few days, they had it down. They performed it for Donna when she stopped by one afternoon on her break. She said it gave her goose bumps.

On Friday afternoon, she stopped by my house for a glass of wine after school, and we sat around the dining room table, shooting the breeze, laughing, gossiping. All in all, a very good week. I even got paid. However, because I worked only two days Thanksgiving week, my check was a paltry $540. I would not get paid at all for the two-week Christmas break. Obviously, I was too poor to buy presents for thirty-six children, so I decided to make them a treat that related to our healthy eating unit: homemade granola, "guaranteed to build muscles and enhance beauty and health."

I baked batch after batch, then put hefty servings into Ziploc bags. I copied the recipe onto an index card. Across the top, I drew a sun and moon and the motto, "Good for breakfast or a midnight snack..." I made thirty-six copies of the card and stapled one recipe to each bag so the kids could make it for their families if they wished.

I asked permission to use the lunchroom for a cooking demonstration and taste test, but my mentor told me it was against the law. She also said that it was against board of education policy to provide any food to the students that was not "commercially packaged" and warned me not to give out the granola. I decided to proceed as if I never heard a word she said.

Our performance day finally came. Most of the kids had Santa hats and wore red and white. Freddie wore sunglasses and a red fedora and had something up his sleeve. They looked great. I felt nervous, but they couldn't wait to take the stage.

Kayla started with an original poem about the birth of Jesus, which probably broke the law three different ways, but oh well. Then Pierre lead the group in "Melody from Heaven," then came "The Night Before Christmas Rap."

I had brought a small floor tom from home and a couple sets of drumsticks for DeVille and Joseph. They had been practicing in school and out, and their chops were tight. They did more than keep a righteous beat. They actually talked to each other through the drum. When their arrangement called for a pause, they put up their sticks like army guys.

Whoever had a verse stepped up to the mike, said their part, then returned to line in some signature fashion. The cheerleaders did splits. Kyisha and Pierre dirty danced and Tyrese shimmied. The audience hooted and hollered.

But it was Rap Master Freddie who brought down the house when he walked on stage for the last verse in his hat and shades. No one noticed or cared that his verse was totally out of sequence. He had star quality. He was exciting. He ended the song by screaming into the mike, "Do your thang! Do your thang!" and "Put your hands up!" with a call-and-response with the audience, "Whoo whoo," "Whoo whoo." The crowd went wild. "Now SCREAM!!!" he capped it off, and the audience screamed like crazy. DeVille grabbed the mike and shouted, "Give it up, y'all, for Room 118." Deafening applause. The class left the stage in a dancing, jumping, jubilant tumble to a standing ovation.

They had established a reputation for themselves, one they could truly be proud of. They were a big hit. They did it all themselves. I was very proud of them.

"I hope you'll be taking that drum home now," the vice principal said. "I'm tired of hearing that racket all day long."

The children's voices singing, "Melody from heaven, rain down on me, rain down on me," echoed in my head all weekend, making me smile. I recognized a strange feeling I had: happiness. I was happy! After months of hard work and discouragement, a reward at last! Working on my lesson plans over the weekend, I felt anticipation instead of dread. I looked back over the months and realized that maybe we were building something after all. What it would turn out to be I still didn't know yet. But something was beginning to take shape.

The end was a flurry—a Christmas party in the room. We pushed the desks back and made a dance floor. We blasted CDs and tapes. We cut the lights and enjoyed the pale natural afternoon sun of winter. There was lots of slow dancing. We had a few snacks that people brought but not many.

At the end of the day, a box of pre-wrapped presents came from the office, labeled "boy" or "girl." Charity gifts for poor kids. The children were familiar with the ritual from Christmases past. "Bootleg!" they derided the gifts, though they were winter hats, scarves and gloves in assorted colors, brand new with the tags still on.

I handed each student a package of homemade granola and sent them off with wishes for good health in the new year. Some tore into it dry, though I implored them to wait to try it with milk at home, me assuming there was milk in every refrigerator. Tyrese proclaimed it "good."

"Got any more?" he asked, checking his muscle for results.

Destinee crabbed, "Coconut makes me throw up," and looked disgusted and disappointed. This from the child I'd spent hours making a tape of Stevie Wonder songs for. "Well, you can't always get what you want," I told her. "Just try to be gracious about it."

Honestly.

Andre lingered and helped me carry things to my car. After the last load, I turned to thank him. "Well, about all I can say is *merci beaucoup et joyeux Noël!*"

He smiled. I knew he was still working on his French because the phrase book was missing. He looked across the street, and I thought he was watching some kids across the way. But he was thinking. Wheels were turning in his mind. He turned his gaze back to me and said, with bravado and a big smile, "*Adieu, mon professeur.*" I had not taught him that. He did that all by himself. "*Très bien,*" I told him. "Nicely done. *Adieu, mon ami.*"

And off he went across the snowy parking lot, past the dumpsters with the seagulls perched on top, hunkered down against the winter wind.

Chapter 21

So Far

I was trying to collect my thoughts for a TV show taping. It was an education-themed interview show hosted by Vernon Jarrett, a well-known Chicago writer and black historian I'd worked with on the *Sun-Times* editorial board.

I suspected he'd ask me what I'd learned in four months as a teacher. I made a list:

I learned that you can't teach every child, as hard as you might try.

I learned that every child's learning style is different. Whatever they cannot do one way, they can probably do another way and you have to identify and build on that.

Class size is a key indicator of success or failure. Too many children can diminish expectations. Thirty-six children were too many in one class.

The internship program was great in theory, spotty in practice. Interns' experience depended not so much on the school or the students as the support the interns received from the institution and their mentors.

I learned that whatever you planned to do would take twice as long as you thought.

I learned to buy the expensive, heavy-duty stapler.

I learned that no matter how many times a teacher has explained something, it was not as effective as showing. Neither was it as effective as letting students do for themselves. Even then, it didn't hurt to explain or show once more.

I learned you have to be fair. I learned that nothing seems fair to seventh graders.

I learned to seek out other teachers for feedback and advice. They were generous.

I learned that staff meetings in education are like hostage situations.

I learned that educators often speak to adults as if they are children, which is annoying.

I learned that the school secretary would make a most excellent administrator.

I learned how important parent support is to a child's success in school. I learned to keep parents informed, to always be happy to see them and to make the most of my time with them.

Before the TV taping, I asked the assistant principal for permission slips, so I could take the seventh-grade Christmas show video. I was so proud of them and thought they ought to be on TV. She said she didn't have any forms, but she'd ask the principal. Later, she said she asked, but he said no. "No what?" I asked. "Just 'no'," she said.

The communications director for the board of education, who'd set up the program, rolled his eyes when I explained why I didn't have the tape.

He also asked me why I hadn't been in the paper lately. I told him I got heat last time. He was incredulous.

The last opinion piece I'd written had appeared in October. I heard through the grapevine that a certain principal had "a hissy fit" when he saw it. He never said a word to me about it, but my mentor said she spoke for him in informing me that any works submitted for publication "had to be approved beforehand by the principal and district office."

I told her I'd like to see that in writing with the signature of the person who had given the order. And that was the last I heard of that. Still, who needed the grief? Was it worth it to stick my neck out, go to the mat for the First Amendment? Was it good or bad for my students to see their teacher's picture in the paper, writing about our experiences? You could argue both ways.

Veteran teachers knew the drill. It's infinitely easier to say "no" or "we can't do that" or "you can't do that" than it is to go forward with new programs, to support new ideas or personal initiative. That is why teaching, while it attracts creative people, also frustrates them.

There. Another thing I'd learned.

Chapter 22

The Mid-Winter Lull

I was away from them, but they were with me.

Conversations and events replayed in my mind. I worried about them, what they were doing with themselves with all the free time on their hands. I wondered if anyone's parents had gotten them books for Christmas, as I'd asked in a note I sent home before the holiday. I knew Kayla would make it through her latest, *A Tree Grows In Brooklyn*. I checked it out of the library for Kayla at Mary's recommendation. I'd see Mary on TV and in the paper, all out there, kicking butt and taking care of business, and smile at her secret connection to a girl she had never met but cared about deeply, because she was growing up just like Mary had—poor, but sustained by books.

I took down the Christmas tree in record time. It was a relief. My faith was tightly focused in my day-to-day work and bolstered by the hope of the world embodied in the babe in the manger. Yet still I felt caught in the trap of Christmas materialism, in terms of things I couldn't afford and didn't get for people who already had so much.

Because it was the longest we'd gone since the beginning of the year without seeing each other, it occurred to me what a privilege it was to know these students, to see them every day in their lives away from homes and families. I humbly realized that my own children's teachers had long known them in the context of their independent lives. They knew things about my children I didn't know, just as I knew who slow danced with whom at our Christmas party.

I resolved that when I called parents, I would make one good call (congratulations on your science fair winner) for every bad call (your child is misbehaving in class and derailing the education of thirty-five other kids).

I planned the curriculum for our return: the founding of the U.S., the Constitution and Bill of Rights, geometry and pre-algebra, wrap up healthy eating, then a weather unit for science, poetry and a new novel, *The Outsiders*, for language arts.

I wrote an e-mail to friends and relations I had horribly neglected while becoming a teacher.

The good news: I'm still standing. Someone told me that 'if you make it to Christmas you're a veteran. Congratulations. Of seven Teachers For Chicago interns that started the school year, three of us remain.

I have 36 seventh graders, including many foster children, five students with learning disabilities, one student who is autistic. I am the third-shortest kid. Our days are chaotic, frustrating battles of will, interspersed with moments I can only describe as divine grace. Some learning has been detected. We have read two novels, learned to read maps and the stock markets. We are speaking a little French. However, we are still forgetting to capitalize the letter "I" when used in the first person. We were a big hit at the Christmas show with our brilliantly ad-libbed rap of "The Night Before Christmas." We also swept the seventh-grade science fair.

My family is well and happy. Natalie is in the decision process for high school, Mia is her usual upbeat self, Artie is his usual laid-back self and I continue my adventure in humility. Keep us in your thoughts in the New Year and light candles for Room 118 as the Iowa Tests approach in the spring.

As the return to school grew closer, I started feeling anxious. I felt soft from all the time off, not wired and "combat-ready." I should have copied more stuff at Office Max. I should have written weeks' worth of lesson plans. I should have... I felt frustrated from going to the Field Museum and the Shedd Aquarium, seeing the treasures there that I could not share with my students because of the field trip prohibition. But I met another teacher who was a docent in a fantastic percussion exhibit, and he told me he came to schools and did percussion workshops. I got his information and wrote a memo to the principal asking permission to invite him to work with the seventh graders. I handed him that memo on three occasions but never got a response. Eventually I gave it up.

The downside of being ignored was that it cheated the kids. The upside was that if I was in trouble, I no longer heard about it from the principal. Speaking of whom, one morning a girl from across the hall ran up to me, breathless, and shoved a piece of colorful mail into my hand. It was a mailer from a Gary, Indiana, Lakeside Casino.

"Look," she said.

On the cover was an arresting picture of our principal. His first name was over his picture. Under his head shot was the caption: "Big Winner!"

Chapter 23

The Second Half

"**W**hy don't we do math anymore?" they challenged me. Anymore? We'd been back to school like ten minutes and already the crabbing had begun.

"We do math," I told them, "when we read the Dow Jones industrial averages, or the year-to-date precipitation, or do our healthy eating stuff—that's math. When we do science experiments, that's math. And we're not going to stop with the graphs until you speak it like a language. You must learn to organize data and present it articulately."

They looked at me like I was a complete dunce, which I had always been when it came to math. I could always count on my students to exploit a weakness. I taught math by studying what I had to teach, the night before I had to teach it. If I forgot it during the night, I'd study it again the next morning before school. If someone challenged my methods, I handed him or her the chalk and let them teach it "their way." All roads led to math. It was the only fair way for us to proceed. As we began the second half of our year together, we were multiplying and dividing fractions and working with decimals. Geometry was on the horizon.

And then a strange thing happened. Someone came to observe our class. It was a reading resource teacher from the little kids' building. I think it had something to do with an upcoming review by the state board of education. Or maybe they were building a case to give me the heave-ho. The assistant principal made a threat in the direction of the latter, when my class got on her last nerve in the lunch line.

We'd had a relatively successful morning, did some handwriting in French, worked on our healthy food project a bit, then moved into two science project presentations. The center started to come apart at the bathroom, and they were a disorganized blob of protoplasm and fists in the lunch line. I was rounding up stragglers like a border collie and policing the line when the assistant principal sent them back to the classroom with a threat of "no lunch!" This had happened once before, but the principal overruled her on grounds that it was against the law to deny the children lunch.

With much griping and moaning, we returned to the room. The assistant principal followed to tell us how sick she was of Room 118, how she could always tell when we were in the hall and that we were a disgrace to the entire school. Then she asked me to clear some "good" people for the lunchroom and said that the no-goods were to eat in the room. I kept about a dozen. Time passed and I sent someone to ask how we were to get lunch in the room.

My messenger reported back, "No lunch."

I went to the office and found the assistant principal behind the counter.

"I guess you've come to plead their case, but I don't want to hear any of that crap," she told me, loudly. She went on to tell me that my students needed a brand of discipline that I was failing miserably to deliver.

"I am not here about any crap but a point of law," I told her. "The last time this happened, I was told it was illegal to deny the children lunch."

"I take full responsibility," she said, "because I'm an administrator."

"Just so we're clear on that," I said, taking my leave.

I wolfed down a sandwich in the teacher's lounge and got the other barrel unloaded on me by the gym teacher.

"I'm not much of a fan of your program," he informed me. "I don't think anyone should be in the classroom until they're certified. I think you take away certified positions. I went through the regular program, student teaching, and I think you need that to know how to handle a classroom."

"I can appreciate that," I said, knowing that part of what he said was true. I did not have the strength to argue that no one was taking away "certified positions." The Chicago Public Schools filled hundreds of chronic vacancies each year with uncertified teachers. Low-performing schools tended to have the highest numbers of uncertified teachers. Schools with the biggest problems had the most vacancies. That is how I happened to be there, not by knocking a certified teacher out of some imaginary employment line clamoring at our schoolhouse door for a job.

The assistant principal entered, still fuming, and slammed a Lean Cuisine into the microwave.

"Bad day?" asked the gym teacher.

"Terrible," she said.

"Maybe you need to get rid of four or five students," he offered.

"Maybe I need to get rid of four or five teachers," she growled, storming out of the lounge. Ouch. But I saw her point. I might have felt the same way if I had to be the editor for a bunch of rank amateurs who couldn't spell and punctuate.

Seven interns had started the year. Three of us were left, including Astrid, who had shown more fortitude and resourcefulness than I had given her credit for. I knew she was smart, but I didn't think she was that tough. She was holding her own with the sixth graders, a motley yet cunning crew, given to violence and stealing. Many things she had bought with her own money (she had paid out of pocket that year to outfit two different classrooms due to her transfer) had disappeared from the classroom.

The most recent intern defector struggled mightily to hang on until Christmas.

"I'm in therapy, I'm on Prozac, I'm getting the hell out of here," she told me at the Thanksgiving assembly. She thanked me for the Aerosmith picture I gave her in October ("This is your focal point...") and said it helped her hang on a little longer. Her fourth graders got a new teacher in January, a relative of an administrator, who settled in with daily help from our mentor, though she was not in our program.

I did not begrudge the interns who left. In time I would see others come and go, some like the white-flight victims of the neighborhood a generation before, who moved out in the middle of the night. The pain and shame of leaving was a personal and professional defeat for the fledgling teachers. They had started with the best intentions to help kids, not to hurt them. Some never came back to claim their supplies. I was hanging on by my fingernails day to day, hour to hour. I knew how precarious we all felt.

Experienced teachers told us not to be so hard on ourselves. "Write off your first year," they said. "It's a lost year." One extraordinary veteran teacher admitted that her first year "felt like being in a dark cave."

"It wasn't until the second year that I began to see shapes around me," she said, "and at the end of the second year I started to see light at the end of the tunnel."

Of course teachers who took the traditional route and had student teaching experience were more qualified as rookie classroom teachers! Those of us who came to the profession through the fire as interns with little supervision or guidance seemed to learn everything the hard way. We made just about every mistake there was to make. But that was no excuse to write off an entire year. According to my count, I wasn't the only one having a year. There were thirty-seven, soon to be thirty-eight, years going on in our classroom. That is practically a lifetime.

Robert, who had noticed the way teachers came and went, asked me, "Mrs. B., you can go back to your old job any time you want, right?"

"Absolutely not," I told him. "I am your teacher today. I will be your teacher tomorrow and every day for the rest of the year."

Tyrese, angling for a day of frolic with a substitute, forced the issue.

"Mrs. B., when are you ever going to be absent? Your hair is almost totally gray, you're old. C'mon. When are you going to miss a day?"

"Never!" I told him in my witch voice. "I will be here to torture you every day!"

For good measure, I threw back my head and cackled like a lunatic. He shook his head and rolled his eyes at my dementia.

Chapter 24

Hip Hop 101

Students weren't allowed to bring headphones to class, and it hadn't been an issue until one Friday at the slushy end of winter, when I had to tell several people to put the headphones away. I realized it was not a sudden epidemic of headphones; they were listening furtively to a tape player being passed desk to desk at the fringes of the class.

Finally, I seized the headphones and the tape player and put them in my desk drawer.

"Can I get that back at the end of the day?" Racquel asked. Aha. So she was the owner. Interesting. Someone who usually followed the rules was breaking them that day. I was curious about what was on the tape. It had been more interesting to my students than what I was trying to teach. I decided to check out the competition and take the tape home for the weekend. I gave Racquel her tape player and headphones with instructions to leave them at home in the future.

At 7 a.m. Saturday I was sitting in my robe, drinking coffee and grading papers at the dining room table. I slipped the tape in.

"Pussy on the floor, pussy on the floor, spread your legs. Pussy on the floor, pussy on the floor, I got a big dick."

I sucked a sip of coffee into my windpipe as my head whipped around so my eyes could bulge at the tape player, as if I had to see it to believe what I was hearing. Sure enough, the "song" continued.

It was rap, with a drum machine beat and a keyboard pecking out one note at a time. Horrible basement quality production, kindergarten musicianship, words triple-X raw. The second track had rhyming words.

"Hold up, wait a minute, let me put my dick up in it..."

There were about ten songs, and every one was about sex or violence, in the most base, lowbrow terms imaginable. One was a string of insults: "You look like shit. Your mama look like shit. You smell like shit." How hard is it to rhyme "shit?" Who were these rappers who didn't even think to try?

The tape appeared to be a commercially-produced cassette, a major label release by a group whose name I recognized. But the material was such utter swill, it didn't make sense; those guys were on the radio and TV, this stuff could never get airplay. Or was there some new, looser standard operating? Had I become a prude? True, it startled me at red lights when someone in the next car had the windows down, subwoofer vibrating the trunk lid and a rap mix blaring "mother-fucker," "bitch" and "kill." Maybe I was "out of time," as the Stones put it.

The household started to wake up when I got to the track "Bald-headed coochie rat (your hands can't touch that)." I hid the tape like an ugly secret. When my husband left for work, I slipped it into his pocket. "Give this a listen, will you?" I asked. "I want to know what you think. Ask the other guys at the shop, too."

The guys who work at the drum shop were all drummers. Some were rock 'n' rollers who spent years on the road. Some were young guys who played in bar bands. As working musicians, they understood the power of music, its ideas, its commands, its sway. They weren't exactly sisters of the convent. They were not easily shocked.

The phone rang in the afternoon. It was the drum shop boys. They were howling with laughter, screaming. The tape was blasting in the background. "No way!" I heard guys shout. "This is insane!"

"What is this shit?" my husband asked. I explained that it was a tape I took from a student. "You've got to be kidding me," he said.

"Did you listen to the whole thing?" I asked.

"No, just the first song."

"Keep going," I urged. "Call me back."

When they called back later, their initial shouting and hysteria had diminished to moaning. Wave after wave of shock and insult had worn them out, like swimmers in the surf. Tommy, though, grabbed the phone and cracked that his band, The Buckinghams, wanted to cover "Hold Up, Wait a Minute."

Kevin, who was a senior in high school, got on the line and apologized to me.

"What are you sorry for?" I asked him. "You didn't do anything."

"I'm sorry you have to teach kids who have been exposed to shit like that," he said.

On Monday, I asked Racquel about the tape. She confirmed that it was not the music of the artists whose name appeared on the cassette, but a "mix tape" that had been recorded over.

"You can't tape over a pre-recorded cassette," I argued.

"Yes, you can." The kids were amused that I didn't know the trick with a piece of tissue that made it possible to record over commercially-produced cassette tapes. As usual, they were minding each other's business and had joined in the conversation. Everyone wanted to tell how to bootleg a cassette. Not everyone wanted to talk about what was on the tape.

"Mrs. B., you listened to the tape?" Freddie asked.

"Yes, I did," I told them. They were embarrassed. They glanced away, at each other, down at their feet, then looked at me expectantly.

"You know me, I like songs about loooove," I said. "That tape made me feel slapped around. It was depressing. I heard zero musicianship, no poetry. The images—I can't even call them ideas because there was no thought—were ignorant. It was all insults and hate and disrespect. I didn't like it one bit. It was like music for people who hate themselves and everybody else, even the people they have sex with."

"Yeah, but it was raawww," Freddie said, gesturing with his hands out and up and his knees bent, head and body bobbing like a video rapper. The others laughed.

"Shocking is easy. Ideas are hard," I said. "What do you think Marvin Gaye or Stevie Wonder would say about that tape?"

"They'd say it was shit!" Cortez blurted, dashing behind Eric so I couldn't tell who said it.

"You're doggone right," I said. Discussion over. Now, what to do with the tape itself?

Racquel and three siblings lived with their great-grandmother and two cousins. The mothers of the children (who were sisters) and their mother (Racquel's grandmother) were all "on the pipe," was all I'd heard. Great-grandmother was doing her best despite poor health. It was hard for her to get up to school, but she did. On parent-teacher conference day, she climbed the steps to visit four or five classrooms. The oldest kids, teenagers, were giving her trouble. It was hard to keep them in line. She worried about child welfare taking all the children away if the older ones got into trouble with the law. She didn't want the family broken up any more than it already was.

"I pray every day that I live long enough to raise these children," she said. Two generations of women between hers and her great-grand-children's had fallen down. She had stepped up.

Did she need this weight added to the load she was already carry-ing? I didn't think so. So I told Racquel I couldn't give the tape back in good conscience, unless her great-grandmother knew about it. I would return it if we all sat down and listened to it together.

"No, Mrs. B., why?" she whined, horrified at the prospect.

"Grown-ups are nosy. It's our responsibility," I said.

"Please don't call my grandma, Mrs. B.," Racquel begged. "I don't want that tape back. You can keep it."

"I'm gonna burn it."

"Yeah, whatever."

Chapter 25

Bottoming Out

Overwhelmed, exhausted, sick, jealous, lonely, irritable, despairing, I realized it must be late February, the shank of another Chicago winter.

I felt like a robot. The alarm went off at 5:45. Shower. Read the paper. Pack lunches. Get dressed. Go to school. Do battle. Come home. Do homework. Check children. Fix dinner. Go to college. Come home. Fall into bed. Fridays and Saturdays, I slept twelve or thirteen hours a night. That had been the routine for the past six months. I had no social life. I had no time, no energy and no money for a social life. It was a rare event that got me out at night. Twice I got dressed up and started out, only to turn back, too exhausted to go through with it.

What did I have in common with my old friends anyway? One sent me a note that he'd written a novel. Another sent his first-place short story from a fiction contest. On the rare occasion that I had time to turn on the television, there were my old friends and colleagues holding forth. It was jarring, surreal, suddenly being in a new world, an anonymous member of the public who went through voice mail hell instead of having the straight-through number and someone on the other end happy to hook me up. Had I really been out with these buddies just nights before, drinking beer and talking politics? Their public presence was part of their workday. Mine was far removed. I would come to call this my Deep Underground Phase.

The rock critic was throwing a party for his new book. The bash didn't start until 10 at night. Three bands were playing. One was a Black Sabbath tribute band called "Black Stabbath." I couldn't miss that one, so I took a nap and threw a folder of ungraded worksheets in the garbage.

Looking at my old friends' busy, exciting, media lives, part of me was ugly jealous. I was sad, too. I missed them. I was achingly lonely sometimes, so needful of adult companionship and their irreverent perspective. We used to have lunch a couple times a week. We talked many times during the day. Now, I had virtually no adult contact during my working day. Now I wolfed my shitty little lunch from home in seventeen minutes while I policed a bunch of crazy kids in a smelly, deafening lunchroom. Cortez would sometimes swipe me a milk, when the lunch lady wasn't looking. It was his way of taking care of me, a tiny show of kindness, and I was grateful for it. I left thirty-five cents at the lunch lady's window.

Stuck in a rut as I was, it was a rare treat one Friday morning to get a break in my daily routine. I'd been asked to speak to high school journalists at their annual convention at my university downtown. I asked my mentor if she would supervise my class while I was gone.

"I don't sub," she replied.

After I explained that it was only for an hour, then she could deliver the students to the library, she relented.

On Thursday, I told her their homework had been to rewrite the first three paragraphs of the *Declaration of Independence* as a "Dear John" letter to King George. They would read their versions aloud for her the next morning.

"Whoop-de-do," she said.

I arrived at school mid-morning after my downtown speaking engagement, uncharacteristically dressed in a business suit and heels. The children were happy to see me, waving and calling to me from the library line, highly complimentary about my stylish look. They usually saw me dressed like a commando: pants, flat boots, simple top. (I admire teachers who wear dresses, heels and hose and accessories to school. I don't know how they manage. I could not do the job dressed like that. I was on my feet all day, up and down ladders, jumping on chairs, chasing down kids, moving around. My perfect school uniform would be a one-piece industrial uniform, one of those pants and shirt combos with buttons or a zipper up the front and lots of pockets. Either special forces khaki or CPD tactical officer black would work, color-wise. Chemical spill containment suit white would not. Combat boots and earrings would complete the ensemble. If I were superintendent, I'd offer them free to all teachers.)

Since it was Friday, the afternoon went down the drain in its typical fashion. Every week had a Friday. Why did every Friday have to be so messed up? By afternoon they were noisy, inattentive, irritable and generally horrible. Tyrese said "motherfucker" out loud just to see what I would do about it. I shrugged my shoulders.

I was so frustrated and sick of them that I screamed at poor Carlos, who had merely gotten up to ask me if he could go to Ms. Gamble's class to get something he left there. I tried calling him twice over the weekend to apologize but got the answering machine. I didn't leave a message.

The following Monday morning was freezing and rainy. I had realized over the weekend that I had an appointment with my new doctor that day. I booked the appointment in late January, but since he only saw new patients one day a week, it took me a while to get in. When I got a reminder message on Saturday, I realized I'd have to take Monday off from school, and I had left nothing behind for a substitute. I felt bad that whoever walked into my classroom would have to wing it.

At 6 a.m. I phoned the substitute teacher center, protocol for when a teacher was absent. The sub center was a central routing office at the board of education that matched substitutes to vacancies and dispatched troops. It was not easy to get substitutes at our school. I met a woman at a party who told a horrific story about subbing in a first grade classroom at a school where the kids ran wild and the office was so rude and uncooperative that she walked out at 1:30, got in her car and drove away, never to return. I asked her the name of the school. You guessed it—my school.

I continued to get a busy signal at the sub center. I redialed every couple of minutes. I toyed with the idea of going to school at 8 with my lesson plans, teaching until it was time to go to the doctor and leaving an organized day (at least on paper) for whatever victim they rounded up to take my class. Nah. That day, I would be just as unprofessional as those I criticized.

Still busy at 7:30. I got through to the school office at 7:45 to let them know I would not be in. I told the secretary that the phones at the sub center must be broken, that I'd been getting a busy signal for nearly two hours.

"That's normal," she said wearily. "Keep trying."

Still busy at 8:55 a.m. Still busy at 9:11 and 9:15. Schools were already in session. I felt ashamed to work for such an inefficient and uncaring bureaucracy. I felt a rising indignation and with it, a sense of justification for my guilty day off. I felt I owed the system nothing, no courtesy, no loyalty, no support, nothing. On my sick day, I was sick of all the adults who worked for the school system who barely tried to do their jobs even marginally well—sick of the lot of them, absolutely disgusted with them.

The sub center line was still busy at 9:30. It was still busy at 10:30, when I left for the doctor. I called the school secretary back. She said they had someone to cover my room, and I didn't have to call the sub center any more.

I reminded myself as I drove through the gray mist to the doctor's office that I didn't work for "the system" or even for the bungling adults who operated it so poorly. I worked for the children.

I wondered what was going on back in the classroom. I knew that if a stranger was sent, the only reasonable expectation was preserving life and limb. The only other time I'd had a substitute, it was a man, a big man, who became so frustrated by the end of the day that he shoved Tyrese and choked Eric. At least that's what the kids told me. The man was never seen again.

I heard from an aide that the Friday before, during my hour-long absence, my mentor had the class sit silently and copy out of books. They did not read their *Declaration of Independence* interpretations after all.

"You could have heard a pin drop," the aide said admiringly.

Fear, intimidation and copying out of books. That was precisely what I was learning at college not to do. That was not learning, that was a bunch of crap, we were told in our teaching classes. Yet these methods were revered at my school, where quiet and order were prized.

It was little comfort that a review team from the state, after spending a week at our school conducting eighty observations and interviewing fifty teachers, recommended that the teachers do more hands-on and small-group teaching, more critical thinking activities. They criticized the staff for leaning too heavily on in-the-seat direct instruction and worksheets.

The state team also interviewed students. The findings: "Students complained about people acting out in the classroom, talking and yelling out and throwing paper. They said they don't feel anyone listens to them when there's a problem."

I felt gratified that both times our class was observed we were doing hands-on, small groups and critical thinking. It was noisy, but we were on the right track, according to these experts. But the validation was little comfort to me in my bottoming-out phase.

I was told that bottoming out happened to all first-year Teachers For Chicago interns at some point. It comes at different times for different people.

I'm sure some of my bottoming out was due to a chronic, escalating lack of respect from the principal. Before the meeting with the state examiners, for instance, an aide ran to fetch me, breathless. "The principal is calling for you. You'd better get over to the library right now!" What was so all-fired important? He wanted me to take notes as the state team presented its findings.

Ironically, the only paper I had to take notes on was an envelope, marked "confidential," containing a referral from the principal to a classroom management course at the teachers' academy. The course conflicted with graduate school, but my mentor said I could be fired if I didn't obey my principal's order.

I typed up the notes during my prep period and delivered them to the principal early in the afternoon. He asked, "Where is the rest of it?" I assured him that the state examiners' comments were complete. "Where's my part?" he asked peevishly. He wanted his reaction to their comments, a corny basketball metaphor of the students dribbling down court and the teachers as a team and how what we did determined whether each student made the hook or the jumper, hit the three or missed the easy layup.

My mind reeled. I fled the office, saying something over my shoulder about how I'd work on that part over the weekend and be sure to add it. Back in the classroom, I picked up rumblings that one of my girls was pregnant. Hints and innuendo were flying around the room. I saw Sherika pat her belly and smile. God, no, I thought, the motherless child pregnant at twelve? It was too much. I put it out of my mind to think over during the weekend.

At day's end, aliens abducted the vice principal. Someone charming and upbeat claiming to be her came on the intercom told us to have a nice weekend and go straight home. At 3, a half-hour after dismissal, I was called to the office to pick up my check and told to go home. I was the only teacher left.

"Even the Lord rested on the seventh day," sighed the sympathetic alien who had assumed the vice principal's physical shell. She reminded me that she had been at school all the previous weekend preparing for the review team and was ready for some R&R. Pretty crafty of the alien to throw in those details. A convincing performance.

As part of my bottoming-out phase, I sent mayday messages to people who had offered me help in the past. One offered encouragement; another suggested I was being set up; a third promised to send some classroom management techniques. I never got them.

I also reached out to former colleagues, apologizing for my "deep underground phase."

"I used my editing skills last week," I told them. "I had the kids write letters to U.S. Education Secretary Richard Riley protesting his proposal to cut summer vacation to one month. One young man closed his letter by telling Riley that he was 'a bogus piece of monkey crap,' and 'Have a nice day!' with a smiley face. I wrote in the margin in my teacher red pen, 'Antwan, I'm not sure it's a good idea to call the U.S. education secretary a piece of monkey crap. Think you can reword that?'"

I tried to explain to the people I had been so close to just six months before what had become of me, but it was like trying to make contact from the afterlife. It was impossible to convey how exhausting it was working with children, how they sucked the life out of me and fought me every step of the way but needed me at the same time because school was the most positive, consistent thing in their lives. I had flashes of memory, but no words to describe the small moments that revealed to the kids the big world beyond our ugly little corner or the beauty in front of us where we stood.

I felt like Robert DeNiro's character in *The Deer Hunter* when he returned from Vietnam to his small Pennsylvania steel town, where life had gone on as usual. "I feel a lot of distance," was how he put it.

Chapter 26

No Coincidences

One time I interviewed Alice Walker, and she said something that stuck with me. She said there are no coincidences, only markers on the path to let you know you're going the right direction. After that, I never saw coincidences again, only markers.

It was a cold spring day, the slush had melted and my car was running rough. I dropped it off at the shop after school and walked the mile or so home. Because I was on foot, I found markers right there on my path. Tons of them.

When my girls were little and we'd walk around the block, we'd keep an eye out for evidence of the "rubber band fairies." We'd find rubber bands left by the people who drop off mailers at houses. We always found at least one or two, sometimes piles of them. Sometimes red, other times blue or beige, sometimes large ones, sometimes small. The kids would take them home and do Barbie's hair with them.

Coming home from the car mechanic, another fairy had been at work: The Twistie Fairy. For blocks, every 10 feet or so, I'd find another blue twist-tie. Nelson used them to make his moveable creatures and he called them "twisties." Just that day he had asked me if I had any twisties, and I did not. When I spotted the first one I laughed out loud and bent to pick it up. As I put it in my pocket, I saw the second one, and another after that.

I must have looked like some sort of nutball as I gathered them up. Burdened down with my teacher bags, I'd walk a couple of steps, stop, bend, pick up another blue twistie. By the time I got home I had a whole bouquet of them, probably 50.

"Look what I found!" I crowed to my children as I came in the door, holding out my blue bouquet.

"Twisties for Nelson!" they hollered back. They were impressed with my haul.

I thought of Alice Walker and our interview in her suite at the Ritz Carlton. The memory seemed dreamlike and long ago, but the wisdom in her words was immediate and clear and real: There are no coincidences.

God is with us, always, in the smallest moments, in silence, even in discarded twist-ties someone threw in the street, making a trail as he walked along, not really thinking at all, certainly not thinking that his discarded trash would mean anything to someone coming behind, anything at all. Yet for the person following the path, it was proof that I had not been forgotten. I was not alone.

Not long after that, something happened to my friend, Fred Dobrinski. He played guitar in the band with my husband for years. Later, he went back to school and became a music teacher. After a few months at his suburban Chicago school, he learned that there was a long-forgotten "instrument room" behind a locked door in a nondescript hallway near the auditorium. He went to take a look.

He must have felt like Howard Carter discovering King Tut's tomb when he unlocked the door. Inside were thirty-five guitars. Not trombones, not snare drums, not violins. Guitars. Another friend, a businessman and guitar aficionado, paid for repairs and cases, and Fred added guitar classes to his curriculum. It was no coincidence. Neither were the gift certificates from Borders which would surprise me later on. Neither was the marker I found on the sidewalk at the end of the year, one I almost did not see through tears and nearly stepped on and squashed.

Chapter 27

Pierre

Whenever there was an ugly crowd on the verge of danger, Pierre was there. In a fight between kids swinging two-by-fours I tried to break up after school one Friday afternoon, Pierre was at the center of the brawl, stripped down to his t-shirt on a winter afternoon, howling at the gray sky, screaming at the top of his lungs, stoking up the crowd.

There had been a terrible fight between two girls after school another day. One was hospitalized with stab wounds. The other was in the juvenile detention center. Tragedy, all the way around. At that fight, Pierre was ringside. Others were accessories after the fact; they helped hide the weapon.

Pierre seemed to have radar for violence and usually insinuated himself into it somehow. He liked to instigate it, too, by being argumentative, manipulative, volatile. He was also sensitive, loving and articulate. He was complex and fragile. I cared for him and worried about him. I was glad to see his mother when she stopped by school.

"I am concerned about Pierre," I said. "He seems to be on a self-destructive track, but he has so many gifts. He spends a lot of energy stirring up conflict with gossip and insulting people to start fights. A fight is one thing, but I'm worried he's going to shoot off his mouth to the wrong person and get himself hurt. He doesn't seem to realize that his mouth can be a dangerous weapon."

I asked Pierre's mother whether he'd ever received counseling, and she said no, but she'd certainly agree to it. She was at her wit's end with him. She said she'd come to school the next morning to talk to the guidance counselor with me. She didn't show.

But I told the guidance counselor that Pierre's mom had agreed to counseling, and the counselor said she'd arrange services. Soon after that, a social worker visited the mother. She reported back to me that Pierre would get counseling. Bless her. Bless her.

Because of the help, though, something drastic happened. It was discovered that Pierre lived outside the boundaries for our school.

"Is this your mother's house or your grandma's?" I asked him, pointing to the address on a school form.

"My mama," he said.

"But I thought you lived with your grandmother."

"No. I live with my mama," he assured me, clueless that his honest answer would get him booted from our school.

The die was cast.

Tuesday afternoon, an office aide dropped Pierre's transfer documents on my desk. I filled in the information about how many days he had been absent and tardy all year. I shook his hand and wished him good luck. That was it. He was out.

"Good luck at your new school," I told him. "Keep working hard."

The next morning, Pierre was back, sitting in the office. His mother was behind closed doors with the vice principal.

"I didn't think I'd see you again," I said.

"I'm here about the fight yesterday after school."

Like I said, if there was trouble, Pierre would find the middle of it.

A few minutes later, he left the office looking like a whipped dog. His mother screamed, "This is the motherfucking last straw! I swear you belong in a mental hospital."

I ran after them and caught Pierre at the door. I handed him his portfolio of schoolwork.

"Thanks, Mrs. B.," he said. And then he was gone, a split-second silhouette against the bright morning sun before the big metal doors slammed shut behind him.

Pierre had had many difficult days in our classroom. But he had great days, too. I would never forget him. That part was true. He would always be on my conscience.

I felt like I had palmed him off on someone else, like I had passed the buck. I wondered whether I should call his new school, tell them he was approved for counseling services. I would ask the guidance counselor what, if anything, had been lined up in terms of transition services.

One afternoon the following week I heard a familiar voice behind me say, "Hey, Mrs. B."

"Pierre," I said, "how are you? How are things at your new school?"

"I'm not there yet," he said.

"But it's been a week," I said, "you haven't been in school all this time?"

"No, we needed three forms of ID," he said.

An office aide on guard duty at the door interrupted.

"You are no longer a student here, Pierre, you can't go walking through the school…"

"The children will be out in a minute," I told him. "I'll tell them you're right outside. Take care."

The difference between life and death. That's what Haberman said school was to some kids. A week had passed and Pierre still wasn't in school. Had I pulled his lifeline?

Chapter 28

Spring Planting

The class planned a seed-planting project. It was part science, part sentiment. It was important to me that they take home something living that would sustain them. Any garden is a celebration of life and a symbol of hope, and my hope was that they would become nurturers and caretakers, that they would assume responsibility for tending to living things. I hoped they would take from our classroom living connections that would keep growing after our time together was over. I hoped for surprise when the seeds sprouted and delight at that small yet significant success. They voted for cucumbers, melons and tomatoes.

We saved our milk cartons at lunchtime until we had two or three for each student. Our wide windowsills with the afternoon sun would serve us well. I bought potting soil with fertilizer pellets and packets of seeds.

It was chaotic and messy, but we managed to get the crops in. I showed them how to read the packets to know when we could expect to see sprouts popping up from the dirt. They looked at me doubtfully. Urban gardeners are hard cases. They were doubtful that windowsills crowded with milk cartons would soon be a garden.

We also decided to plant sunflowers all along our window wall outside of Room 118. We'd been studying the poems of Langston Hughes and decided to name our garden in memory of the poet who knew despair but held fast to hope. I picked up a wooden garden marker in the shape of a sunflower, which Nate painted yellow and green. He added in yellow on black in the center of the flower: Langston Hughes Memorial Garden, Room 118, C/O '01.

Exhausted and buying time to get grades in for the third-quarter report cards, I rented *The Mighty* for the class. The only movies we watched that year were *The Witches* and *The Outsiders*—after we read the books. But since *The Mighty* was about writing a book, with a powerful message about courage and chivalry, I let it roll.

This touching coming-of-age story is about a boy with a fatal disease that makes him need leg braces and crutches. He is assigned to tutor a great big strong kid who has a learning disability in reading. They become friends. Max becomes Kevin's "legs." They identify with the Knights of the Round Table and do honorable deeds because that is what knights do. The movie is divided into six "chapters," and while the ending is sad because Kevin dies, Max learns to read and ends up writing his own book. It ends with Max considering the meaning of the "once and future king."

"That can either mean he can come again, or, when someone so great once was, someone so great will always be."

The kids talked so much during the movie that I could not tell whether they were watching or listening. Three bodies wrestled for space in the big chair. I was amazed when they burst into applause at the right moments. I was doubly amazed when Sherika, who at the beginning of the year was practically illiterate and who talked more than anyone, recited word for word the advice Kevin gave Max in their first tutoring session: "Every word is part of a picture. Every sentence IS the picture. All you do is let your imagination connect them together."

It was Sherika again who found the perfect verse for our Langston Hughes garden marker, from his poem, "Motto."

I play it cool
and dig all jive
That's the reason
I stay alive.
My motto,
As I live and learn is:
Dig and Be Dug
In Return.

My mouth dropped open, I ran up and hugged her. The double meaning of "dig and be dug" for the garden knocked me out. Her wheels were turning. I proclaimed her an intellectual heavyweight. She took a bow.

In the middle of all this, the third quarter came to a screeching halt, which meant report cards—a crushing task. I agonized over grades. It was my first time doing report-card pickup solo. When the parents came for first-quarter grades, the four seventh- and eighth-grade teachers met them as a team on the auditorium stage. Second- and fourth-quarter report cards went home with the students. Third-quarter pick-up was a day-long open house for conferences with parents and students.

It took place in our classroom, which was looking pretty spiffy. Our March weather chart covered two walls. Every day we noted the high and low temperature and our artists made suns, clouds and snowflakes to mark conditions. The thirty-one-day chart showed that "March comes in like a lion and goes out like a lamb." Samples of the kids' work hung everywhere: letters, haiku, graphs, maps and colorful tessellations (pattern repetitions) from geometry.

I had three kinds of cookies and apple juice, a video screening area so parents who missed the Christmas performance could see it on tape, portfolios of every child's work, a Langston Hughes poem and a letter pleading for the return of borrowed paperbacks and textbooks. Twenty-three parents showed; thirteen didn't. I was told that wasn't bad at all.

Freddie's mother left with a big smile on her face after seeing the Christmas video. Carlos' mother was pleased because his grades went up. Racquel got a terrible report card, which was way out of character. But she vowed to bring up her grades in the last quarter.

I had a list of books on tape at the library for Nichelle's grandmother, so she could build on Nichelle's great listening skills to help her become a less reluctant reader. She vowed to get the books so Nichelle could read along with the tape. Kayla was a no-show, and that was strange.

At the teachers' lunch break, I heard that the Mad Crapper had struck again. A turd on a paper plate had been left inside the teacher's lounge refrigerator the day before. The refrigerator stood empty after that.

Chapter 29

Bad Things Happen in Threes

It was strange, very strange, that Kayla didn't come for report card pickup. She had not been sick. She didn't come to school for the rest of that week. When she was absent again the next week, I called her house but the phone was disconnected. I asked Racquel, who lived down the street, to stop by. She reported back, "Kayla's out of town."

Another week passed. How long could she be gone, this girl who never missed a day of school? Where had she gone? Her family was so poor she hardly had clothes on her back. Where on earth could they be?

Toward the end of the second week, the school secretary came to the classroom and said a police officer had been inquiring as to Kayla's whereabouts. I told her what I knew and gave her an accounting of when she had last been to school and how long she'd been absent.

I became alarmed at the "missing" reference. The policeman explained that an aunt had filed a missing persons report for Kayla, her mother and sister. We searched Kayla's locker. Empty. All of her schoolbooks and four novels from our classroom, including my personal copy of *The Outsiders*, were stacked neatly in her desk. No notebooks. No paper.

She was gone, and she had known she was going. That much was clear in an instant. I turned every book inside out thinking a note might fly out. I flipped through pages looking for clues.

Nothing.

Our last conversations had revolved around a special book I bought for her. It was a book of short stories written by an author who shared, almost, her name. I was reading it first to make sure there was nothing

132

glaringly inappropriate in it, but mostly so we could discuss the stories, reader to reader, as we had all year.

"When I'm done," I had told her, "it will be yours to keep."

Seeing the book on my nightstand drove me to tears. I was frantic with worry, sick at heart, grief-stricken. Was she safe? I prayed she was. I prayed that she would come back to us, her friends since she was little and her teacher, who believed in her and loved her. You are not forgotten, I whispered to the air often as the days passed. Still no Kayla.

Finally, after another week, the guidance counselor informed me that Kayla was safe and that she was with family members in another state. For reasons that were not revealed, mother and daughters had left.

This sort of thing happens to kids and families every day. The reasons that send them fleeing could be homelessness, domestic violence, debts, drugs, gang threats, who knows? Things get out of hand, intolerable. Leaving becomes the only option. It broke my heart that she had to endure whatever situation had become so drastic that there was no other answer.

There was no address for me to contact her yet. But I vowed I would find her. I would get an address. We would write letters. I would let her know she was missed and pray for her return.

I realized how I had come to depend on her, and it made me feel even worse. She had supported me, while she had dealt with perils she never revealed.

She had been a young woman of dignity and character who supported others when her own world was crumbling beneath her feet. She had been my strength and my encouragement, a seventh-grade girl. No wonder books had been her escape.

The honest questions that a teacher must ask were brutal. Had she felt she couldn't confide in me? Did she distrust me or think I was insincere? Had I been such a weakling that she didn't want to burden me with another problem? If she had asked for my help, could I have helped her?

At the end of April, the guidance counselor told me she had an address and promised to forward a package. I bought the stamp and a bubble envelope. I stuffed the book and a note inside:

Dear Kayla,

I hope this letter finds you well. I am happy to learn you are in school, though I am envious of your new teacher! You were a presence and a positive influence in Room 118, and we all miss you very much! Tyrese and Freddie are keeping me busy, but I'm not having many book group conversations.

Here is the special book I promised you. I hope you enjoy it. Short stories are such a delight—so much variety in a collection, so much to think over. Take it slowly and give each one a chance to sink in.

I just finished *Holes* by Louis Sachar. It won the Newberry Award in 1999. It's about a boy who gets sent to boot camp for a crime he did not commit. Their punishment is that they have to dig a hole every day, five feet wide and five feet deep. It is very funny and adventurous. We are reading it in class now.

We all think of you. Stay strong. I give thanks every day that my first year as a teacher I had the good fortune to have you as my student.

With love,

Mrs. B

On an impulse, I threw in a medal I had bought in Rome a year before, an enamel of *La Madonna della Strada*, the madonna of the streets, on a gold chain.

God would look out for Kayla, I told myself. She was his child, not mine, and her faith was mighty. Drawing on her example, I chose to believe that I would see her again someday.

Pierre was in the hospital. Word had it he had been attacked in an abandoned house. Several versions of what happened were floating around. All sounded like the neighborhood ghost stories about kids getting "snatched" and dragged into abandoned houses. But Sherika said Pierre's mother called her and told her the whole story and that she was going to visit him that afternoon.

At dismissal, the vice principal came on the intercom and told teachers not to let anyone leave, to keep the students in our classrooms because of a "serious incident" outside the school. There was much grousing, "Awwww," and "You can't make us stay," and other such nonsense. Two teachers hurried past. I poked my head out in the hallway and asked, "What's up?"

"Shooting outside," they whispered.

It was bound to happen sometime. Now it had. Protect the kids.

"I don't see anything outside, let's draw the blinds," I told them. I turned off the lights. I picked up *The Outsiders* and started reading out loud where we'd left off.

Ten or fifteen minutes later, another announcement told us that we could dismiss the children and told the children to "go straight home."

I added to that before walking them out.

"This is no joke. There was shooting. Keep your wits about you. Look sharp. Pay attention. No alleys. Main streets only. Move fast. Go straight home. I'll see you tomorrow."

The story was that two guys without guns were running away from two other guys with guns. Shots were fired. The two unarmed men ran through an open door into the little kids' building, where they sought refuge. Asked what they were doing there, they refused to leave (and be shot at again) and stalled for time, talking loudly and posturing in the hallway.

The alleged gunmen waited outside, across the street.

Someone called the police, and the gunmen ran off when the squad car pulled up. The police arrested the two guys inside the school.

It didn't bother me at first, but that evening at college, I found myself crying before math class and again in the bathroom during the break and again on the way home. It was so overwhelmingly sad and stress-ful, the shooting and Pierre all in one day.

∞

Due to the circumstances, Pierre's transfer was reversed, and when he got out of the hospital he came back to us to complete the rest of the year. He never went a single day to the other school, because the adults in his life could not pull together three forms of identification and organize themselves to register him.

He was subdued. He seemed weary. The first thing he told me was that he'd been in the hospital. I said I'd heard, and he could stay after school if he wanted to talk. I gave him a hug and told him his desk was where it always had been. He found his chair and settled in at his old spot near the door.

After school, we sat on desks in pale gold sunbeams of spring light that made everything seem soft and fuzzy.

"How does it feel to be back?" I asked. "Are you okay?"

Pierre said he was in the hospital for one day, and he had to get two shots. He said the guy approached him as he walked down the street, asked him if he wanted some wine. He told the man he didn't drink. The man asked him if he had any dope. He told the man he didn't use it and didn't sell it. Then the guy grabbed him by the shirt and wres-tled him into an abandoned building. Pierre was harmed, but fortu-nately, some other men arrived, and they held the assailant until police arrived. Pierre had already been to one court appearance and would have to go again.

"My mother cried," he said.

"I'm so sorry," I told him. "Life is hard enough without that kind of sadness and trouble."

We sat a while longer, talking, until it was time to get going.

"I'm glad you're back," I told him. "We really missed you."

I hugged him goodbye.

"See you tomorrow," I said.

He'd been out of school for exactly one month. His whole life had changed.

Chapter 30

"Remediation"

The Monday after the Mad Crapper left a turd in the fourth-grade fish tank, my intern liaison from downtown showed up at my door. "Hi, come on in," I told her.

But she was not there to observe. She had been summoned to an "emergency meeting" about Mr. Diaz and me.

"What's going on?" I asked.

We were both in the dark. There hadn't been any major blow-ups or notorious incidents of late. Nothing out of the ordinary, just business as usual. Something urgent was afoot, though. When the principal called her, he said it could not wait until the next week. It had to be that day, first thing in the morning. She canceled her appointments and arrived first thing that day. She cooled her heels until 1:30.

Mr. Diaz was summoned first. I was called at 2:20. Waiting for me around a conference table in the principal's private office were the principal, the assistant principal, the liaison and the mentor.

I was handed a piece of paper with "Intern Remediation Plan" printed in bold letters across the top. They informed me that I was "in remediation" and the paper was the plan for how I would correct my shortcomings.

If I failed to meet the "desired outcomes," I could be fired. It would be up to the principal whether I stayed, was shipped out to another school or kicked out of the program altogether.

Desired Outcomes:

1. Establish ways to discipline students rather than escalating the problem; review discipline policy and techniques.

2. Exhibit professional behaviors and practices; be receptive to criticism and admit mistakes rather than make excuses. Be able to see yourself objectively.
3. Exhibit professional behaviors and practices; develop and maintain organizational techniques to create a conducive learning environment.

Time line for attaining the desired outcomes: two weeks.

The principal detailed specifics of my shortcomings: poor discipline in the hallway; not walking students all the way out the door at dismissal; allowing students to go two at a time to the washroom unsupervised; using inappropriate language; failing to say the Pledge of Allegiance and sing both anthems every morning; failing to read every morning from 9 to 10 a.m.

I was flummoxed. This was crazy! Everything was in slow motion. When he stopped talking, I heard my own voice.

"What about this 'being receptive to criticism and not making excuses'? This implies I am an excuse-maker and possibly delusional. I think we need to have specifics—not innuendo—on the record."

Silence.

The principal assured me, in clipped tones, that "someone" would be observing me, perhaps on a daily basis, perhaps more often than that. The sheet said my fate depended on his assessment, that he himself would "observe evidence of discipline techniques, organizational behaviors" and "observe and document professional behaviors and practices" in order to make his decision.

My mentor would "give guidance and ideas related to discipline and managing student behavior" and "assist with arranging, organizing or analyzing the classroom learning environment."

I wanted to pound the table and demand where all this guidance and assistance had been for the first thirty-six weeks of the school year. But that would not have been professional behavior for a teacher. I wanted to call this what it was, bullshit, but that would have been inappropriate language. I wanted to ask how I was supposed to fix in two weeks what had been set in motion long before, from elements beyond any of our control. But that would have been excuse-making.

So I sucked up. I said, "I welcome the backup. I also welcome whatever feedback you can share with me to help me succeed."

I felt powerless and humiliated.

Before the meeting broke up, Iowa test scores were passed out. Here's how my kids did: two-thirds improved in reading, ten students by more than a year. Pierre and another boy improved nearly three years; Andre, Tyrese and four other kids jumped nearly two years. Kayla was reading at a tenth-grade level. Five went down in reading, including a girl who had a major literacy breakthrough and experienced reading for pleasure for the first time in her life. Test anxiety?

Math was not good. Two thirds improved, but only about ten showed the expected nine months of growth. Ten actually went down.

I made it to the outside door before tears spilled down my cheeks. I would have to play this close to the vest, but I also needed counsel. Donna's door was open.

She was aghast when I told her what happened. She just shook her head and opened and shut her mouth without saying any words for the longest time. She fished the ashtray out of her desk drawer and lit a cigarette.

"They must really want you out of here," she finally said, looking over her shoulder as she opened a window, blowing out a plume of smoke. Her eyes were like hot coals. "Uh, uh. Ain't this the shit."

I showed her the test scores, and she said they were "gorgeous," that I had nothing to feel bad about as far as how well the kids had done in spite of everything, my being a first-year teacher and everything else.

"You know Baldacci," she said. "You gotta go 'full armor' from here on out, just keep going. He won't let you down."

But could He pick me up? I was devastated, flattened.

"Look at the positives," Donna advised. "Look at Tyrese. Look at Pierre. Look at what you were able to do with these kids your first year. There are a lot of successes here."

"Yeah, but what about the ones that did worse?" I asked. "How can you work so hard and have kids not learning?"

"Goddamned Virgo," she said. "Just like me. You obsess over the things that go wrong instead of enjoying what went right."

She paused a moment, then delivered a final bit of advice.

"Girl, don't you worry about that man. He ain't shit."

Late that afternoon, I phoned Tyrese's father with the news that he had tested at grade level in both reading and math. After the months of struggle, the happy ending choked him up.

"That sure is good news," he said thickly. He decided not to tell Tyrese the news, merely ask him questions about how he felt he did and what his expectations were. He'd let Tyrese learn his scores for himself.

"I guess I'm going to have to get him that new pair of Jordans he's been asking for," he said, breaking into a chuckle.

The next day, Donna handed me a laminated, card-sized copy of the famous drawing entitled "Jesus Laughing." It is a simple pen and ink of Christ in a most uncharacteristic carefree pose of delight and mirth.

"I just love that picture," she said. "You hang on to it. Keep it handy."

"Do you think he is laughing at us, at the silly, pointless games humans play against each other?" I asked.

"I think in the middle of all he knew and witnessed, he still managed to be joyful," Donna said. "He wants us to be joyful."

Chapter 31

Assumptions

Being on remediation did not preclude me from giving a talk to the office of accountability staff downtown at the board of education.

I touched on the insensitivity of assumptions when I faced the bean-counters who defend standardized test scores like they are the holy grail. They, same as most policy-makers, like things to fit in neat little boxes. Wrapping themselves in comfortable assumptions makes it easier to defend their hard and fast policies.

I told them the story of one kid, a fair student, who tanked the Iowa test the year before. On test day, he took the garbage out before school and found a dead body in the alley. His mother sent him to school after he finished talking to the police.

I told them of a pattern I'd noticed about test anxiety, one I hadn't been able to locate any clinical research on but that might make an interesting study someday. Two girls I thought would score highly on their Iowa tests did terribly. According to their scores, they lost two years of learning in reading. I knew the scores were dead wrong. Test anxiety? Maybe, but why? They were smart girls who did fine work, thoughtful readers who had experienced breakthroughs. Later, I learned that both were rape victims.

Try as we might to consider the conditions that children come from before they pass through our doors, we cannot anticipate everything and therefore should not assume anything.

Even as I spoke to the accountability staff at board of education headquarters, I could not assume that I would be a teacher much longer. I might be fired in a couple of weeks, depending on the outcome of my remediation plan. The chief of accountability seemed to think my plight was silly. He laughed it off, told me not to worry.

But one thing I had learned was to challenge my assumptions. With my background, I thought I would automatically look for the story behind the story, not take things at face value, greet developments with a raised eyebrow and a "Hmm." But I got out of the habit, somehow, or maybe I was so bombarded with new developments that face value was all I could deal with for a while. I had assumed everyone had milk in the refrigerator at home. I wasn't thinking that witches and evolution would offend anyone's religious sensibilities.

Teachers, especially white teachers with middle-class backgrounds, must challenge themselves not to fall into the lazy habit of white privilege. For instance, when I arranged for a student to take a dance class at half-price at my dance studio, half was still too much and transportation was out of the question. The frustration over the lost opportunity felt worse than no opportunity at all.

We learn from such mistakes.

Michelle told our college cohort about an eye-opening incident at an open house at her school. She'd had a problem with a boy in her fifth-grade class who was always fooling around. His reading skills were exceptional, she said, but he goofed off in class all the time. She was loaded for bear when his mother came for an open house.

The boy arrived leading his mother by the hand up the stairs. She was blind. By the other hand he held his two-year-old brother. He settled his brother with markers and paper, instructing the little guy to stay put while he and their mother talked to the teacher. Don't forget to put the caps back on the markers, he reminded his brother.

Michelle had handouts that needed parent signatures. The boy read all the paperwork to his mother, then helped her sign them.

"All this time I thought he was 'irresponsible,'" Michelle said. "Now I realize that in school is the only place he can act like a ten-year-old kid."

Sarah had a story about another boy, a seventh grader, who showed up at a school located in a public housing project at the start of the year. He was in line for breakfast every morning at 7:30 and spent his days attending classes.

Someone finally realized he wasn't enrolled and found out why: The boy had been on his own since his mother had gone to jail for a drug offense in late August. He heard that police and social workers were looking for him at his old school and worried that he was going to be put in foster care. On his own, he decided to go to the other school for safety, anonymity and meals.

Once the full story was revealed, the State Department of children and family services was called. Fortunately, an aunt surfaced who lived in the neighborhood near the new school. She agreed to take him in. The boy attended school every day. He read at a ninth-grade level.

"This is what school means to these kids," our college professor told us. "It's their safe haven. So when you find out what chaos these children are coming from, consider where they have been when they have a hard time settling down to learn in your classrooms."

When she taught first grade in a western state, she had one student who came to school every day reeking of urine. She figured he was a bed-wetter and was angry at parents who would send a stinking, dirty child to school. Other children held their noses and refused to play with him. What she found when she knocked on the door of the family's home was a young immigrant mother, whose husband was a migrant worker. She was trapped at home with seven tiny children. The first-grader was the oldest. There were four in diapers. There was no washer or dryer in the apartment. At night, everyone threw their dirty clothes in a corner. The diapers went there, too. Every morning, the first-grader pulled clothes out of the pile and went to school.

The mother welcomed the teacher into her home. Her English wasn't so great, but no matter—she was elated to see an adult. Who knew how long it had been, with all of her family in Texas and she confined and isolated with seven little children? How could anyone move all those babies, and the family's laundry, on a bus to a laundromat?

The teacher called human services to obtain a washer and dryer for the family and contacted the landlord for the hookups.

"You never know," she said.

You never know.

Chapter 32

Livin' On the Edge

My Teachers For Chicago liaison came for an observation, to see if order had been established in Room 118 in the nick of time to get me out of hot water.

It had not. I was "livin' on the edge," a situation in which, Aerosmith observed, "you can't help yourself from falling."

At the time of the observation visit, I was working with small groups on their plant projects. We were measuring and graphing the growth of our seedlings. It was time-consuming and hands-on. The room was stifling, thick with humidity and the full blossom of summer.

Our window garden was lush and green. Some plants stood four inches tall; ambitious cucumber vines were climbing up the screens. Some kids were working well at their task, and a small group was creating a bright green bulletin board with completed graphs, empty seed packets and photographs of our planting project. Others made a show of working at the garden but were actually sabotaging other kids' plants, opening the screens and pushing them to their deaths over the edge of the windowsill. After school, I found about a half-dozen milk cartons and their spilled contents on the ground outside the window.

Destinee and Sherika decided it was a good time to do Eric's hair in braids and worked at it noisily, gossiping like beauticians at a salon. Eric let out occasional yelps as they combed, parted and pulled his hair into the new style. I told them to end it and get started on their plant graphs, but they paid me no mind.

One of the undocumented realities of the school system's overemphasis on Iowa test scores was a backlash: Once the tests were over, many students, especially in the upper grades, quit working. The test was what they worked toward. After tests were done, and certainly after the results were in, the school year was over as far as they were concerned.

In my conversation with the liaison, all I could do was admit that my students were acting worse than ever, because I had failed to bring them under control. One of my remediation tasks was to "be receptive to criticism and admit mistakes rather than make excuses." I did not offer excuses. I flat-out admitted I had failed to control these children.

The principal, who was to "observe and document" my progress, had eyeballed me in the hallway a couple of times, but there were no formal observations. The loose oversight in the wake of the dire threat seemed to confirm that my remediation was a paper set-up. The individuals involved would always be able to point to those papers and say I was a lousy teacher.

My mentor, who was to "give guidance and ideas related to discipline and managing student behavior" and "assist with arranging, organizing or analyzing the classroom environment," helped me take my class to the washroom a couple of times and spelled me for an hour one afternoon, so I could play in the faculty basketball game, which gave me an insight I would never forget.

No one knew I could play ball. But thanks to coaching girls' teams for three years, I managed not to embarrass myself on the court. These opportunities for bonding with kids are vital for building connections. They need to see us in many roles, as guides on field trips, as voices in the class choir, as teammates on the court. We'd had pitiful little opportunity for that. All week after the game the eighth-grade players high-fived me in the hallway, "Good game, Mrs. Baldacci!" We should have played every week all year long, I realized forlornly. An opportunity lost.

At the end of two weeks, I got called to the principal's office to learn my fate. He said I'd made progress. However, I would remain on remediation through the first quarter of the next school year. The "results" column of my remediation form said the same thing in all three boxes: "Somewhat successful at meeting desired outcome, there is still need for improvement. Remediation will continue through first quarter of 2000–2001 school year."

The non-resolution left him with the power—and all-important paperwork—to fire me whenever he felt like it.

I stated that I felt that he should honor the timetable—the one that he himself established—instead of leaving me with the sword of Damocles hanging over my head. No, he said, this is what the professional educators on the team believed I "needed." It was for my own good.

Almost as an afterthought, he informed me that I would be teaching second grade the following year. I assured him I would do my best.

I walked back to my classroom with conflicting emotions. We had filled out wish lists and I had asked for seventh grade again, feeling I could do better now that I knew the pitfalls. My second choice was sixth grade, my third choice fourth. Being sent to second grade, clearly not what I desired, looked like a punishment. This is what others with greater experience felt was best for me. I said the same prayer I'd said the year before, "Thy will be done," and accepted my fate. But not without beating myself up a little bit first.

Had I been such a dismal failure with my seventh graders, self-contained in the largest classroom in the school with all of our personalities and problems? Surely someone else would have been a better teacher for them than I was. Was it criminal to leave them with me all year? Would I be equally as dismal with second graders? What other students would be sacrificed to my ignorance and inexperience? I was having a regular pity party. My eyes were watery with tears.

I blamed myself for every child who didn't do better, for the ones I failed to reach, who clung tightly to their contempt for authority and learning. I had asked the seventh graders to write down one thing they learned that year.

Some said they didn't learn anything. One said he learned to "smoke weed and drink." One said she learned how to plan her dream trip so she can travel when she is older. One said her teacher had told her that she saw something special and beautiful in everyone in our class, and she was trying to see people that way, too.

Just then, on the sidewalk, I nearly stepped on a clover chain I had made on the playground that morning for a little girl whose name I did not know. I picked it up and thought of Alice Walker. Was this another marker on the path? Was it a message from on high telling me that perhaps my place might be with younger children after all? Would that little girl be my student in the fall?

Mr. Diaz was not so fortunate. He was cut from the program. He did not come back to complete his year-end paperwork or collect his belongings.

Chapter 33

The End of Seventh Grade

I had no money to speak of, but I wanted to give everyone a book on the last day of school. I put a $150 price tag on that pipe dream. No way I could afford that. I was looking at a summer of no employment and graduate school. This would be the tightest shoestring our family had ever tried to live on.

I was scrutinizing my bills and noticed a fee on American Express for a program called "Membership Rewards." I phoned them to question the fee and cancel the rewards, which I could no longer afford.

The person on the other end of the line, however, informed me that over the years, I had racked up many points worth of "rewards," which included gift certificates for Borders.

"How much?" I asked.

"You could get three fifty-dollar gift certificates," she said.

"Send them!" I ordered.

Everyone would get a book after all. I had each kid write down a title. Kyisha wanted a twelve-dollar *Chicken Soup* book. Nichelle couldn't come up with a title and asked me to choose for her. Many kids asked for *Holes*, our final novel, which they loved and was the kind of book you could read over and over. Carlos wanted Stephen King's *The Stand*, and I called his mother for permission because it is a wonderful story of ultimate good vs. evil, but it had sex scenes. She signed off saying she'd read it herself when he finished, it sounded pretty good. I agreed and admitted I reread it every couple of years.

The shopping was thrilling. I planned our last days together.

"Sports Day" threw a wrench into our plans. Most of the class was banned from participation, and those who did participate were quickly disqualified for assorted misbehavior such as running away, and sent back to the classroom, sweaty and out of sorts. "Sports Day" was a full day of trying to contain a revolution, apparently.

I had ordered pizza for the class, a luxury I no longer got for my family, and the misbehavers made pigs of themselves, which started off a string of arguments, which led to fights, which got people sent to the office, which—combined with the running away from Sports Day— led to mass suspensions. The vice principal had vowed that anyone who got sent to the office would be sent home for the rest of the year, no questions asked.

"See you in August," she told them as she cast them out with their yellow suspension papers.

"Come back Tuesday so we can say good-bye," I told them. "Come to the window and get your things…"

Between the suspensions and the fact that many children's parents let them take the last week off because it was so hot, we had only about twenty remaining.

We spent our final days stripping the room and watching the made-for-TV version of *The Stand*. On our last full day together, we had a lovely day.

All year long I'd been hearing either, "Mrs. Baldacci, you bring the NASTIEST lunches!" or "Mrs. Baldacci, you have a lot of nerve bringing those nice lunches up in here."

It was no big deal, just turkey sandwiches, maybe with a pickle on the side or a salad or leftovers from dinner at home the night before. I shared my homemade lunches time and again. I even made a lunch for Sherika one day just because she asked me to and no mother ever made one for her. I brought cucumbers often for Freddie. He loved them. Racquel swapped me a bag of flamin' hot Cheetos for my sandwich one day.

Trying to organize ourselves for a last-day feast was futile. Some wanted Subway. Some wanted pizza. Some wanted McDonald's. Nothing was resolved. I let it drop and decided to bring mass quantities of stuff to make our own "Mrs. Baldacci Nasty Lunch." Smoked turkey, ham, cheese, wheat bread, five bags of salad, three kinds of dressing. Sun Chips. Jars of sour dill pickles. I wrote a bad check at the grocery store.

The kids played volleyball in the morning, using our inflatable globe with chairs as a "net." They danced. They sang. When we did not make any movement toward the lunchroom at 11 a.m., when noon came and went, they started looking at me funny, and I told them we were having a buffet luncheon as soon as we could organize ourselves for a washroom break. We did, without incident. Amazing.

At the buffet, all served themselves and no one hogged. No one threw food. Everyone got enough to eat. There was a minor dust-up in which Destinee and Cortez hurled horrible insults at each other, but other than that, it was quite pleasant. We whiled away the rest of the afternoon cleaning up and fooling around with a lot of kids helping paint a mural in the hallway with the art teacher. At 2:30, the bell rang, but no one made a move to leave.

Finally, after several announcements of the late hour, I told them I was going into the hallway to take their pictures as they emerged.

I treasure the series of pictures of them leaving. When I look at them, I hear the echos of their voices in the hallway. They are in constant motion, a blur of color, arms and legs. One of the suspended masses met us at the doorway for a couple of group shots, then DeVille finally kicked the door open and they all tumbled out, screaming and laughing. And then they were gone. The door closed and it was silent. I stood there looking at the closed door, listening to the silence.

"They were here just a second ago. Now they are gone," I thought. "It's over."

It didn't feel like it was over because I still had so much paperwork to complete, and we had one last hour together when they came to pick up their report cards and say goodbye. Then it would officially be over.

For our finale, I had planned to read *Oh, the Places You'll Go!* by Dr. Seuss, give them the newsletters I made for our class, their report cards, portfolios and the books I bought for them on my coupons at Borders.

But I had barely handed out report cards when, at 9:20, security came to our door and rousted us. No final read-aloud. Portfolios and books, which should have been tenderly handed over with ceremony, were palmed off in a rush. After nine months of praying for it to be over, how could I feel so cheated at the end?

I wasn't the only one not ready to call it quits. Andre and Nate stayed for a couple of hours more, just hanging on, and helped me with some records work.

I felt disoriented when I finally turned in my records and left school around 1 p.m.—Piaget's "state of disequilibrium" was in full force. I went home and fixed lunch for the girls and myself. But I still felt antsy, like I had unfinished business.

Around 2 p.m., I drove to Pierre's and Cortez's houses to return the stuff they'd left in the classroom. No one was home at either place; I left their bags on the doorsteps.

Tyrese was suspended, so I still had his portfolio and his book. I went to two wrong addresses I'd taken from school records. Finally, I got his dad on the phone around 2:30 and got the correct address. I'll be right over, I said.

His father greeted me at the gate.

"Tyrese isn't here," he said. "He was here a minute ago. I don't know where he got to."

Just then, Tyrese burst out of a house across the street and came running. I gave him his stuff, told him if he kept his scores up there would be no stopping him. I didn't hug him or anything, because that would have been mortifying, but I shook his hand and wished him well. Even after all he put me through that year, I was proud of what he had accomplished. I shook his father's hand, said goodbye and drove off.

On my way home, I turned on the radio. Bad Company's "Can't Get Enough of Your Love" was on. I turned it up. I looked at the sky. I saw gleaming white seagulls circling overhead in the afternoon sun. I took a deep breath and smiled at the prospect of ten weeks off. Finally, our year was finished.

Chapter 34

Fairyland

"**W**e need a fan. It's so hot you can't believe it. And we need a reading rug where we can gather for stories. They're little, and they need a soft place to stretch out or play. I saw some rugs at Home Depot for about fifty bucks."

My benefactor handed me $100 and wished me good luck in the second grade. I wanted our classroom to be a magical, wonderful, learning place. It would take much more than a fan and a rug to make it that.

Going to second grade meant I was no longer in the old brick building with the high ceilings. I knew no one in the new building and would be starting from scratch, establishing new ties with new colleagues. On my floor were four first-grade classrooms and four second grades.

Due to many vacancies, three of the four second-grade teachers and two of the first-grade teachers were Teachers For Chicago interns.

Though a novice to second grade, I was the "veteran" intern. The two other second-grade interns were just starting the program. Fortunately, one was a young woman who knew everything already. The other was a career changer from the insurance industry. The only certified teacher in second grade graciously assumed the role of our team leader.

Of the two fresh first-grade interns, one was calm and professional, the other had a deer-in-the-headlights look about her. The third first-grade teacher was a veteran who wore sunglasses all day long and complained to anyone who would listen about how she should have been teaching eighth grade and how she resented being sent to first grade by our spiteful principal. The fourth first-grade teacher, Mrs. Todd, was someone who was clearly in her niche, centered and calm, knowledge-able and businesslike about the craft of teaching. Like Donna, she was a woman whose faith was her strength and guiding light in her daily work.

It was odd, indeed, that so many first- and second-grade teachers at our school were rookies. Eight of us, and five were completely untrained. Across the city, most teaching vacancies were in the high-pressure seventh and eighth grades, where the kids are ruthless and the heat to get them into high school scorching. How come our turnover rate was so high for primary teachers, I wondered?

The transient teacher situation had implications that carried over year after year. Many of my second graders were coming from a first-grade classroom that had four different teachers over the course of the year before. I remembered seeing them in the hallways on their way to the art room or the auditorium. They were noisy and badly behaved, running this way and that, slapping each other. Their teachers looked frazzled. A very tall young man who had been a day-to-day substitute took the class for the last months of the school year. He did not come back, though.

A man who had taught fourth grade for part of the year before was in my old classroom, arranging the desks. I poked my head into 118 and wished him a great year. Keenly aware of my shortcomings since reme-diation, I admired the fact that the principal had sent a strong black man to establish order in the seventh grade. Sadly, even with fewer than twenty-five kids, he wouldn't last the year.

I missed the old building as soon as I set foot in my new room, 401. It was on the second floor of the prefabricated, three-story annex next door to the original building. The newer building housed pre-kindergarten through third-grade classrooms. The poured-concrete shell went up in 1978 with a declared life span of ten years. In the year 2000, it had been limping along on its last legs for fifteen years.

Room 401 was painted peach. Acoustic ceiling tiles were missing here and there. Dirty yellow tufts of insulation were visible through the holes. Other tiles were stained from leaks.

I discovered that two walls were magnetic; they would hold posters and student work as time went on. I didn't have much to put up at the moment, since all of my materials were geared toward seventh grade. What I did have to put up, I quickly learned not to hang on the other two walls. They were cold and clammy, sometimes beaded with moisture and defied sticky substances. Posters I hung with sticky-tack one day were on the floor the next morning. I tried packing tape with the same results.

There were three windows, all clouded over from the ravages of time and Chicago weather. Sunlight diffused through them, but we could not see out of them. Only one window opened and closed. Another was permanently fastened shut with screws and bolts. The third was permanently open a crack, its warped metal frame lashed in place with a window shade cord. Any rainfall flooded the metal ledge along the windows. The heating and air conditioning units were housed beneath the ledge, a tragic design flaw that contributed to constant breakdowns and poor air quality. Many of the children had asthma and no business breathing foul fumes and stale air at school. The dampness made me suspect mold was present as well.

The baseboards were rusted through, especially in the washrooms. Teachers sitting on the toilet in their "private" washroom could actually see the feet of children walking into the adjacent boys' bathroom and clearly hear their conversations. Still, the teachers' washroom was luxurious compared to the students'. The girls' bathroom, for instance, had five stalls, but only two were private. Dividers between the other three toilets had been missing for more than a year. Only one girl used the communal three-toilet area at a time, slowing down the breaks considerably.

The easiest part of creating a classroom was the physical, filthy, dirty work: scrubbing the room and bookshelves, organizing ancient books and tossing out the obsolete ones, cleaning cupboards, scavenging tables and chairs from other rooms and stairwells. I had done this same thing a year before, and now I was moving again, into another new house filled with the worthless junk of previous occupants. My only cupboard was half-filled with record albums. There was a record player, but it had no needle.

Getting ready took three days of cleaning, hauling, arranging, hanging things on the walls, fixing broken things. Hauling water was
exhausting but necessary. Every book on every shelf was coated with
dust and grime. The scrub water had to be dumped and replenished
often. My hands ached. I fell into bed when the sun went down and
slept as if drugged until it came up again.

By the time the children arrived Tuesday morning, the room was
clean and cheery with a big blue rug on the floor and a rocking chair.
The fan, placed in front of the only window that opened, circulated
fresh air through the room.

I was satisfied as I looked around. But I realized the hard part would
be making a home away from home that was a living laboratory for
learning. "Patience," I reminded myself.

Everyone punched in and out in the office of the old building, and
the door was open to Donna's room across the hall. She was always the
first one at school.

"My sister," she greeted me. "Are you ready?"

"Not yet," I told her. "I've come for a blessing."

I bowed my head and Donna prayed over me, asking for strength
for the both of us as we undertook the massive job ahead. I tacked on
special prayers for my seventh graders, who would be Donna's kids this
year. We said amen, took deep breaths and went forth to "engage our
students" on the playground outside.

I had thirty-two children's names on my roster, but only nineteen
arrived for the first day of school. It was the earliest Chicago schools
had ever opened, two weeks before Labor Day. Citywide, one in four
children failed to show up for the first day. Chicago's attempt to align
itself with the early-opening suburbs fell flat on its face. The next year,
the system admitted its mistake and returned to the traditional post-
Labor Day opening. In the nation's third largest city, we took the agri-
cultural calendar very seriously.

As I stood in my new spot (marked 401 in fresh yellow paint), the
first familiar face I saw was Carlos. He ambled over, wearing sunglasses,
and I asked him if he'd read *The Stand* over the summer. He said yes, the
whole thing. Then Destinee, Nichelle, Sherika, Freddie and Cortez

came over to say hi, all loud and talking at once. Nearby, some little kids observed them silently. They looked from the big kids to me, back and forth. Joseph walked over to report that his jalapeno pepper plant had borne fruit! Andre, who grew about four inches over the summer, tossed me a "*bonjour*" as he sidled past. I remembered that it was Tyrese's birthday, and I had one of my corny birthday pencils for him. He avoided me on the playground, but I chased him down in Donna's line and gave it to him.

This year I would be the tallest one in the class, I realized as I gathered my new students. Several children's parents handed them off to me directly and introduced themselves. One little girl was handed to me screaming and crying, clinging to her sister, who needed to get to sixth grade. I told the little one not to worry, that we'd have fun and I'd take good care of her until her sister came to get her at the end of the day. She was as tiny as a fairy and quite inconsolable. I finally picked her up and carried her in, sobbing on my shoulder. She hardly weighed anything at all. The baby oil from her face and hair made a blotch on my shirt, above my heart.

The children were eager to get to work. We started our day on the rug, sitting in a circle, telling our names. Some of the boys were James, Brandon, Martin, Hakim, Mario and Louis. Some of the girls were Jasmine, Asophane, Vonique and Diandra. My littlest fairy, the crying one, was named Natasha. Even though she sat next to me, she spoke so softly I had to put my ear to her mouth to hear her name.

We read a *Sesame Street* story about the first day of school, then made a story called "All About Us" on sentence strips that we hung across the front of the room. "Our room has ten boys and nine girls." (We would change the numbers daily in the coming weeks.) "We love to read!" "Our favorite TV show is *Out of the Box*." "Our favorite food is pizza." "Our favorite animals are cats and dogs."

We went over the rules and assigned classroom jobs. I thought lunchtime would never come. We started smelling the food around 10 a.m., but our class somehow pulled the last lunch shift, 12:15, a full hour later than the other second grades. By 11:30, the children were complaining of stomachaches and headaches because they were hungry.

So we had a bathroom break and bought time with a little ballet. I had everyone stand with one hand on the back of their chairs and showed them first position. I put on Otis Redding's "Fa Fa Fa Fa Fa (Sad Song)" and we started our ballet lesson with *demi plié* and *grand plié*. We turned and did them the other way, "just like in a real ballet school." Then we did *tondu* and *dégagé*. When we finished one side, I asked, "What do we do next?"

"Turn around and do it the other way, just like in a real ballet school," Hakim called instantly.

"You are absolutely right!" I said, daring to think that this year was starting off pretty well.

Ballet and Otis tided us over until lunchtime, but I realized we would need daily snacks if we were to survive all year on this schedule.

Lunch went like clockwork. They were quiet in the hallway and kept good lines. I knew this year to walk backward so I could keep an eye on them, or to walk behind them. I told them to stop at the top of the steps. Then I said "pass" and they walked down to the bottom and stopped until I said "pass" again. This is an old school routine I abhor, but it works. One irony of schools is that they're supposed to be places that foster creativity and self-control but instead are paramilitary installations with rigid rules and imposed control.

I sat down with my students at the lunch table, which teachers are not supposed to do for some reason having to do with our contract and our 2:30 dismissal. Teachers and staff want to get the hell out early, so on the books our lunchtime is 2:30. During the children's lunch period, we are "on duty" with our students. Someone decided that being "on duty" meant we stand like prison guards. I decided being "on duty" meant sitting and eating as a family and learning table manners. I always sat down with my second graders.

"Who made you that good lunch?" I asked Mario, the only one with a lunch from home.

"I made it myself," he said.

"What do you have?"

"I have a sandwich, a juice box, some chips, a pudding and cookies. And I have a spoon for the pudding."

"That's a good lunch," I said.

"Here," he said, handing me a chip.

"Thank you," I said.

After lunch we had another bathroom break. Apparently food and liquids go through second graders at a rapid rate. Lunch is only twenty minutes, but the race to the bathroom after lunch was always urgent.

Around 1 p.m., the secretary came on the intercom and said that a Channel 2 news crew and the principal were on their way to our classroom. The year before, a news producer asked three different times to come to my classroom. I refused every request. Why invite disaster? But she had phoned the night before and asked again. I figured, how bad could second grade be? So I told her to call the principal in the morning. I gave him a note to expect a call from the producer, but I was astonished to learn via intercom that he had agreed with the provision that the children's faces not be shown. It would have been much easier to say no, there is too much going on the first day of school, which is the truth. Instead he said, "Why do you do these things to me?" as if I spent my days thinking up ways to exasperate him.

My new mentor came along with the three TV people. She worked with children on one side of the room while I worked on the other. We reviewed alphabetical order and did some more reading. It was nerve-wracking to have the visitors and the camera in the classroom. I felt certain that in the excitement and intensity of day one, I was a blithering idiot. I dreaded watching the piece on TV that night.

At the end of the day, I walked the children out and waited with Natasha for her sister. She held my hand. Hers was tiny, but strong. Racquel was right outside the door, wearing a green plaid skirt and necktie. She'd transferred to a magnet school, and she looked happy.

"How's your grandmother?"

"Fine."

"Did your plant grow?"

"Not very well," she said, "but it's still trying."

She said her book list for eighth grade at her new school included *Holes* and *The Outsiders*.

"I told the teacher I already read these in seventh grade," she said, tilting her head with sassy pride and a knowing smile.

The new interns staggered out, shell-shocked, and felt their way to their cars. I felt their pain. I managed to make it home without driving past my own house, an improvement over last year's first day.

I called Teachers For Chicago headquarters to let the leaders downtown know that the TV piece on "fast track teachers" was scheduled to air on the ten o'clock news. I left a voice mail with one of the men who had been my point person on media in the past.

My own TFC liaison called me a few minutes later. At first she was congratulatory, but it quickly became apparent that she was furious that I had called her partner, who was not my liaison.

"Why didn't you follow the chain of command?" she demanded.

"Well, I've always dealt with him on media issues," I said. "He asked me to keep him updated on anything media-related I did while in the program."

"I wonder if you called him because he is Caucasian. Maybe you feel more comfortable with him."

The conversation, already confrontational and angry, had now taken a turn that left me sputtering, stupidly, "What?"

"I wonder if you called him because he is Caucasian," she said.

"That is ridiculous," I said. "I called him because he had asked me to keep him updated on media things. Are you suggesting that I am a racist?"

"Don't try to put words in my mouth," she snapped.

"Well it sure sounds like that's what you're saying. Is that what you think?"

Meanwhile, I was thinking that "Caucasian" is such a weird word. I kept saying it over and over in my head. "Caucasian." "Caucasian."

"This is not about me," she said, "This is about you."

The conversation was going in circles. I felt sick and off-kilter. I apologized for my thoughtlessness, and told her that in the future I would follow the chain and that nothing like this would happen again.

"Oh, I'm sure it will," she said.

"Oh come on, that is totally unfair," I argued. "I said it wouldn't happen again, and it won't happen again."

"We'll see," she said, hanging up on me.

Back on the shit list, I thought, and it's only the first day of school.

I was heartsick about the way this thing had broken, mainly because there was some validity in what she said. Why had I called the white man (the "Caucasian") and not her? Was there more to it than the fact that he had been my point man on media? In my previous career, I'd dealt almost exclusively with white men in power positions. That was the power structure I cut my teeth on. That was what I was familiar and comfortable with. I had worked for and with white, black and Latina women and been an editor myself with authority over men and women of all races. But always, white men held the highest power. Had I failed to learn a key lesson about operating in my new profession, which was vastly matriarchal and minority (yet with a white man in the top position)? It seemed terribly complex and confusing, more than I could grasp on the first day of school.

It was arrogant to proclaim "I am not a racist" without taking time to think, "Am I?" So I went to church and prayed on it a while.

I searched my heart with questions about racism. I didn't have all the answers. I liked people for who they were. My favorite downtown liaison was Frank Tobin, not just because we were neighbors and I'd known him longest, but because he seemed to be a kindred spirit. He was the reason I'd walked through the door of the program in the first place. He had used the words "vocation" and "social justice," the same words I had secretly carried in my heart as an unseen hand seemed to propel me in a new direction. He was always encouraging and kind and always took time to talk to me. Just that week, he had mailed me a wonderful article from *Harper's* about the failure of public education being a government conspiracy to keep in place a service industry of undereducated people in dead-end jobs.

Then again, maybe it was easier to feel close to him because his feedback was positive. The most encouragement I ever received from my liaison was that she felt I had "the potential" to be a good teacher. She never said I was doing anything in particular right. She never sent me articles in the mail she thought I'd enjoy.

I wondered whether my sin was vanity rather than racism. Maybe I connected better with people who affirmed rather than criticized me, which is human nature.

In the end, I was grateful to my liaison for forcing me to face that ugly question. She was not kind and we did not love each other, but she was a good teacher to me that day. She opened my eyes. She taught me to question my motivations and alliances. She made me think. I left it at that for the time being.

I had a case of nerves all evening. By 10 p.m. I was in the bed, hiding under the covers. The piece aired after the first commercial. I peeked out and watched it with one eye. To my immense relief, it was fine. Thanks to skillful editing, I was not a blithering idiot. Carol Marin smiled and that's money in the bank.

No more media, I told myself. I would not do anything but teach those second graders to the best of my ability, every day for the rest of the year. It was best to lie completely low, fly under the radar. I was still in remediation, after all, and my fate lay in the hands of my liaison and the principal, both of whom I'd managed to piss off on the first day of school.

Chapter 35

The More Things Change…

Some things were different in Second Grade Fairyland, but some things were replays of seventh grade. As we found our rhythm that year, I saw the same personality issues, good and bad, the same cases of kids raising themselves, more shocking this year because the kids were so little. I'd see them navigating the neighborhood alone after school, their enormous backpacks bouncing as they crossed streets at a run. Fatherlessness and homelessness were as devastating for seven-year-olds as twelve-year-olds, but the seven-year-olds did not yet have the cunning to act like it didn't matter. They were open about their heartbreak. Sex and violence invaded our days once again.

Most days started in the breakfast line. The United States Department of Agriculture provided poverty-level schoolchildren with free breakfast, and the children lined up for it at 7:30 a.m., a full hour before they needed to be at school. The government and the school bureaucrats realized that kids can't learn on an empty stomach, so in some ways, the lunchroom was more important than the classroom. Despite two significant snowstorms that winter, the schools did not close a single day, because the superintendent feared many children would go hungry. Aside from the rubbery powdered scrambled eggs, there were many yummy breakfast choices: grits, biscuits, bacon, oatmeal and cold cereal, milk and juice. I sometimes bought breakfast and ate at my desk doing paperwork; a teacher's aide delivered breakfast each morning to the principal in his office.

Every child except Mario also ate free school lunch on the USDA. The choices rolled out every week with little variation: chicken nuggets, pizza, cheeseburgers, rarely warm, with canned vegetables on the side. On rare occasions, the kitchen served Salisbury steak or chicken with mashed potatoes and gravy, the sort of institutional school lunch I remembered from childhood.

The cook prepared a separate meal for the staff each day, often chicken, some kind of greens and potatoes. I wanted it, and for two dollars, it was a good deal. But how could I sit down with my kids with a spread like that when they had fish nuggets, a packet of ketchup and fruit cocktail? It seemed unfair and rude, with possible racist overtones in my case, so I continued to bring my own lunch every day in my red lunchbox.

Lunch at 12:15 was hard on all the kids, but it really killed Enrico. Although he was the tallest child in our class, nearly as tall as I was and just seven years old, he was the most immature. The days were long for him. All afternoon he was fretful and asking "When do we go home?" He kicked, I noticed, and tripped other kids walking past his desk.

Getting fed on time was do or die for these little ones. We often had pretzels with mustard for a snack, though Cheeze-Its (the white cheddar cheese kind) were our official favorite. We began carrying a basket to the lunchroom and stockpiling our apples and oranges for the next day's snack. It was good practice because everyone had to pass the basket down the table, not hop up and crowd around it. They also had to add their name to a list with "A" or "O" next to their name. Still, enough people hopped up from the table in our twenty-minute lunch period that I went home every day with ketchup handprints on my back. One habit I never was able to break in the second graders was their maddening habit of patting me for attention. Imagine trying to speak to one child while three or four others are patting various parts of your body and murmuring your name over and over like a mantra.

"Form a line!" I'd tell them. "I'm only one person, and I can only talk to one other person at one time."

I wish I could say I was calm, like Mrs. Todd, but I was frazzled.

So thank heavens for Mario, our class peacemaker. He was calm. He was the first to arrive on the playground every day, scrubbed and well-dressed, wearing a baseball cap and jacket, carrying his lunchbox and backpack.

I hailed him as "The Gandhi of 401" after James threw several fierce, quick punches at Brandon, and Mario got between them before it went any further.

Something did not seem right with James. He was tightly-wound, volatile, and as the oldest, strongest kid in class, seemed on track to be the class bully. I paid a visit at James' house after school the day of the fisticuffs.

It took his grandmother awhile to reach the door. She moved slowly, aided by a walker. I introduced myself, and she invited me in, explaining that James' mother was at work. We sat down in the living room. It was cluttered with medical paraphernalia, boxes of hypodermic needles, blood sugar monitoring kits. The family dog had recently given birth to puppies and the house smelled like a kennel. James brought a couple puppies out for me to see. His grandmother sent him back to the kitchen to feed the dogs. After he put the puppies in the kitchen, I could see his shadow on the wall in the hallway where he hid, listening to our conversation.

I told her about the fight that day and asked whether James had problems at school before.

He had, indeed, she said. He'd spent the previous year in a suburban school, but the problems continued. Now James, his mother and sister were living under grandmother's roof once again and were back at their former school.

The next day, James and Brandon squared off a second time. I called Brandon's mother, and she confirmed that the two boys had trouble in the past and probably shouldn't be in the same class. They shot each other dirty looks from their seats at opposite corners of the room. Invariably, they wound up next to each other in line, ready to go another round. I told Brandon's mom I'd keep an eye on the mood of the room, and see what I could do about separating the two further.

Still, they got into it again on the last day of the week. They started punching each other while lined up for a bathroom break in the hallway. "Freeze!" had worked three times so far at stopping second-grade fights. Thankfully, it worked again. Afterward, James stood against the wall, clench-fisted and trembling, his face a frozen mask of anger, veins standing out in his neck. After all the other students had gone back inside the classroom, I gave Brandon and James a talking-to and sent them to their respective corners.

Before we got busy with "Show and Tell" one of our Friday afternoon activities, Brandon told me he wanted to say he was sorry to James.

"Do you want to do it in private or in front of the class, since the fight was in front of the class?" I asked.

"In front of the class."

"That is so brave," I told him. The children looked on expectantly as Brandon approached James.

"I want to say I'm sorry," Brandon said.

"I'm sorry, too," James said. They shook hands. We all applauded. I hailed them as peacemakers.

If only it was that simple. Second grade was at least as complicated as seventh grade. The peace would not last. New conflicts erupted. Problems from their outside lives came with them through our door every morning, and they were not problems that could ever be solved at school. As their teacher, I tried to teach the art of coping and compromise, which some people believe is the practical path to happiness.

Several of the children were in foster homes, living with a revolving cast of wards of the state, cared for by older women who received about $400 a month for each child.

Many lived with extended family, most often, like James, with their mother, their mother's mother, siblings and cousins. The men of the house were more often uncles than fathers. Three students were officially the wards of their grandparents; one was an orphan whose mother had died the year before of an asthma attack, two others' mothers were incarcerated for drug offenses. Out of thirty-two children, only three came from homes where both biological parents lived together. There seemed to be a lot of chaos at some homes. Louis told me he and his brother climbed in an upstairs window when their grandmother locked them out one afternoon. His brother was in kindergarten. Tashequa called the classroom cell phone nightly, sometimes after 11 p.m. I could hear the television blaring and loud voices in the background.

Family, whatever shape it took, was of supreme importance in second grade. Meeting Mario outside on the blacktop one morning, I asked him what he was thinking about.

"I've been wondering," he said, "why my daddy never comes to see me."

"That's a big thing to wonder about," I said. Without realizing it, I'd begun to parrot the speech patterns of young children. Shorter sentences. Declarative statements. Simple language. Concise questions: "Are you sure?" "How can you tell?" Listening. Letting the children figure things out for themselves. Blocking activities in shorter time periods. Breaking things down to simplest terms.

Mario described a far-flung family of half-brothers and sisters, then came back to his feeling of emptiness about his daddy.

"Maybe when you get bigger you could call him up," I said. "What's your daddy's name?"

He couldn't tell me.

We read a story called *Boundless Grace* about a girl, Grace, who has grown up without her daddy. He lived in Africa. He sent two tickets for Grace and her grandmother to visit him. She visited. She remembered. She was happy. There are all kinds of families, she realized. Not all mothers and fathers live with their children.

That day Mario did not eat his lunch.

"Are you feeling okay?" I asked him.

"I guess I'm just missing my daddy," he said.

He was such a beautiful, well-behaved, thoughtful, helpful, wonderful little boy. He was usually cheerful, joyful, even. His mother was great. A man he called his stepfather came on a field trip but spent the day reading a book. He did not sit with Mario on the bus or partner up with him at our destination.

Despite such heavy baggage, second grade could be as golden and effervescent as a glass of ginger ale. One Friday afternoon, Andrea opened a Sucrets box and announced, "I brought two ants and a roly-poly for Show and Tell." We sang songs every day, Girl Scout campfire songs, "Down By the Bay," "Bingo" and nursery rhymes like "London Bridge" and "Mary Mack." They thought I was a great artist. "Man, she can really draw," they'd say. Every day was a busy day for us.

It was a big adjustment for me to be with young children and so many of them. Since my children were older, I thought I was done with tying shoes and wiping noses, with loose teeth and hard-to-zip jackets. But there I was again. My patience was often stretched and frayed.

It was hard for them, too. It was hard to stay in their seats and hard to wait their turn. It was hard when we had multiple activities going on at once, because everyone wanted to do everything right now. When we played a tape of "Peter and the Wolf" in the listening lab with five sets of headphones, it was too taxing for the other twenty-seven. They couldn't do anything but stage whisper and gesture to the kids in the listening lab about what they were hearing. Louis commando-crawled across the back of the room to the lab and hid under the table. A sympathizer put his head on the table and shared one ear of his headphones with Louis.

They did the kinds of things kids do that make you want to laugh out loud. I laughed out loud, but with no other adult to share it with as it happened, the anarchy in Fairyland reached its full flower of appreciation most often in the retelling. Thank heavens for Donna and my college classmates.

In addition to my new thirty-two, many of my former seventh graders appeared at my doorway to say hello. Pierre ran up behind me after school one Friday and nearly tackled me. He must have grown three inches over summer and he was muscular, more beefed-up than the skinny kid I knew in seventh grade. He seemed good, upbeat.

The girls were awkward, testing. We had a new relationship, one I liked better, to be frank. With no responsibility for their academics, it was easy to listen to them, encourage them. I wondered if it's like that with all former students as the years go by, and I started to realize that it's never finished; it goes on and on. I wondered what relationship I'd have with my second graders in five years when they were in seventh grade, after I'd known them and watched them grow up all those years in between.

I was tempted to harden my heart and dismiss such silly, dreamy nonsense. Such questions assumed that I would remain and ignored the forty percent chance that they would not. Even second graders knew better than to count on people sticking around.

Chapter 36

Cult of Personality

We had been in school two weeks when Labor Day weekend came at last. We were becoming readers and getting to know *Amazing Grace* and Frances, the little badger, and Miss Nelson and Dr. De Soto, the mouse dentist. Every day, we did phonics, handwriting, math, science, ballet, music and citizenship. We were very busy. The new interns, especially the ones who had come from office backgrounds, were freaking out. Managing a staff of adults, no matter how crazy or inept, was scant preparation for the profound range of personalities and non-stop action in a classroom of busy children with unbridled energy. The first-grade intern who looked like a deer in the headlights was missing in action, and a substitute had taken over the class. My mentor must have been busy trying to hang on to the other new recruits, so I just carried on doing what I thought was best. No one came and told me anything, but I didn't expect it and didn't miss it.

The mercury hit ninety-three degrees on the Friday before Labor Day. Thank heavens Natasha's sister picked her up promptly at 2:35 because at 2:40, the air conditioner in Room 401 blew up.

I was walking in the classroom door when there was a loud BOOM! Black smoke poured from the vents. Terrified of a fire, I raced across the room, gingerly raised the lid and clicked the switch to "off." The smoke circled menacingly in the shocked silence. My pulse pounded in my ears.

The engineer was bewildered at the situation. Our unit, broken when I first arrived in 401, had been fixed just a week before. That day another unit in another classroom had blown up. Outside contractors were making a fortune off the board of education to keep these trouble-plagued antiques working. What would happen when winter came and we needed heat?

Even with the air conditioning on high that day, it had been so hot that we did not do much work. The children did not pay attention during *A Bargain for Frances*, my favorite Frances book. There was too much money changing hands and too many plot twists. Only about five children were attentive. We plowed through to the finish in grim determination when we should have savored the exciting tale of treachery. I missed seventh grade. They had loved that Frances story best of all when the little badger helped us learn about characters, sequels and authors' style.

Second grade was sweaty and off track even before a mother and aunt arrived with cupcakes and balloons for a child's birthday. After the cupcakes (and a washroom break, of course) we were so sugared up we could do nothing but twirl around the room in ballet skirts and my old pointe shoes, even the boys.

Louis amazed me by finding a ballet book on our shelf and mimicking positions from pictures. A true kinesthetic learner, that kid, always in motion. I was worried about him because he couldn't read a word. Yet he found so many other ways to learn that he became a teacher for me, a template for multiple intelligences. A year later, he would remind me of songs we had learned in 401 and leap across the room to demonstrate his *grand jeté*. I talked about Louis so often at home that one of my daughters finally snapped, "If you love Louis so much, why don't you adopt him?" She was right: I loved Louis. Both daughters quickly saw why when they came to school with me to help out on occasion. They don't begrudge me the Zip-Lock bag of picture notes from Louis that I keep with their own childhood artifacts.

All that happened over time. On that hot, hot Friday, we were only concerned with surviving until dismissal. By then the birthday girl was overwrought, which can happen from the stress of turning seven. She was mad at me for taking her out of the bathroom line for talking. She was upset when her blue scissors turned up missing. I knew how she felt. My favorite special red stapler had disappeared. I offered a reward for its return, but I held slim hope. It was last seen with Enrico, whom I began to suspect was setting up an office somewhere.

James did not make it to afternoon. He got into so many fights and tiffs that morning that I asked the office to call his home and have someone pick him up for an early dismissal. I was amazed all over again how one serious problem child can run the whole train off the rails.

In the course of the morning, James had reduced three children to tears. Natasha cried so hard I let her sit on my lap in the rocking chair. It was probably against the law or something, but a sobbing child who's been smacked in the face by a bully needs comfort.

Enrico saw opportunity in conflict. He could be fun and silly, but also a meanie and a manipulator with a secret, sneaky side. He and Andrea were the king and queen of complaining. It's strange that children so poor they get free lunches can be so spoiled, too. These two had learned to play adults against one another to get things they wanted. What they really wanted and needed, of course, was attention and consistency. In the absence of those things, they felt entitled to a new toy or treat, or going first or having their way. It made things difficult in the classroom. Their parents admitted straight out that the kids were "spoiled" but stated it as if the children had been born that way, as if "spoiled" was a fact of nature which the parents had no role in creating or responsibility to correct.

There was one child in the room whom I would never call spoiled. She arrived weeks into the school year. She was as tall as me and skinny as a scarecrow. Her hair was uncombed and she often slept soundly with her head on her desk. She could not spell her name. She was not a "new girl." Everybody seemed to know her. She was someone who came to school for a while, then disappeared, later to return. She was my first homeless child. She would turn ten in November, in the second grade.

Chapter 37

Trouble

Hearing James trill, "Hey, look at this," I turned to see him grabbing his crotch and making wildly sexual gestures at the girl sitting next to him. His zipper was down.

I took him out of the room. I told him to zip up. I told him that was no way to act in our classroom. I seated him by himself again.

I sent the necessary paperwork to the office describing the offense, and James spent the afternoon there. He was back in class the next day. I asked the principal what I should tell James' mother about his status when I talked to her that night.

"Tell her to come meet with me on Monday morning," he said.

When I talked to James' mother, I related the problem behaviors: throwing things, hitting people on the head with pencils, punching and slapping other children, repeatedly getting out of his seat and not following classroom rules or directions. He did not complete class-work or turn in homework. When I got to the sexual acting out, she exploded.

"I told him not to do that," she said. "That's what got him at trouble in his old school, touching a girl in the wrong place."

"So this sort of thing has happened before?" I asked, concerned that a pattern might be emerging. Did we have a sexual predator in second grade?

I further learned that James had left our school two years earlier after stabbing a fellow kindergartner in the head with scissors. That year, the kindergarten teacher took early retirement.

Before I could request referrals for evaluating James, I was told I needed to collect ninety days' worth of anecdotal records detailing his problem behaviors in our classroom. That would be Thanksgiving at the earliest. In the meantime, I saw I needed to police James vigilantly, to cut down on wasted time spent tending to children he harmed, breaking up fights and making office referrals. Kids who did not fight back, who did the right thing—"Tell the teacher"—did not see the wrongdoer punished. They didn't understand why he came back day after day acting the way he did.

Late one morning, I saw him furtively stuffing something into his pocket from his desk. I asked to see what he had. It was play money from our math kits, which were kept in a cupboard with a broken lock. He claimed the money belonged to him, that a boy he knew gave it to him on his way to school. The money was not folded in any way. It did not appear to have been carried in a child's pocket at all, certainly not for several hours. I asked the name of the friend. He looked at me blankly for a long pause, then said, "Uh, John."

Later that day, during our bathroom break, a student informed me that "James was kissing a boy in the boy's bathroom." Martin said he saw James kiss Louis, but Louis said it was Brandon.

I saw James touch girls' behinds as they walked past his desk. He choked children, spit in their faces, broke their pencils and rulers, hit them with sharp objects he threw or shot from rubber bands. He wrote "bitch" on a boy's desk in red crayon. He simulated masturbation at a boy from another class in the lunchroom. He rolled up pieces of paper at his desk and simulated smoking a joint. He smashed our collection of ladybugs, which were in a plastic bag attached to the chalkboard.

"Write it down. Keep your anecdotals," I was told when I related the incidents to my administration.

One Friday, James seemed especially wound up. He was loud and confrontational. Around 11:30, Asophane asked to speak to me.

"James has a gun in his desk," she said.

It seemed as if every sound in the room suddenly went silent, then the clatter of the classroom surged up in my ears once again. Asophane was looking up at me.

"Thank you, sweetheart," I told her. "Sit here in the rocking chair, and read awhile."

In my old job at the newspaper there were many wacky, moody personalities, including a few in the running for "person most likely to come in with an AK-47 and blow us all away." Teachers hate to admit it, but we make the same kind of observations in our classrooms. In our room that year, the most likely suspect was James.

I took a quick look around the room, counting heads, seeing where the other kids were, relative to James. He was in the row near the door, halfway back. I decided to approach him from the door side, so he'd have to face me and the wall behind me. His back would be to everyone else in the worst case scenario. I felt cold but calm and under control. Lives depended on what would happen in the next seconds.

I walked over to James' desk, stopped between his desk and the wall, leaned over and spoke to him quietly.

"James, I need you to listen very carefully. Are you listening? Good. I'm going to give you some instructions. I need you to do exactly what I tell you. We'll go one step at a time. Do you understand?"

"Yes," he said, looking up at me, nodding his head.

"Good," I said. "Now the first thing I need you to do is this: Put your hands on top of your desk."

In a split second, he thrust both hands inside his desk and pulled out a small silver object. I put out my hand. He put the gun in my hand. The sound of the room went away again, then surged back as I turned away from him and looked at the small, silver derringer in my hand. It was a cigarette lighter made of metal. When you pulled the trigger, flame came out of the barrel.

I felt weak in the knees and very, very stupid. Why had I expected a child who had not followed directions all year to follow directions in a situation that could have had tragic consequences? I had used traffic stop protocol when the offense called for the SWAT team.

I could have handled it smarter. I could have given him a task elsewhere in the room and searched through his desk. I could have waged a surprise attack, snatching his desk and spinning it away from him, then jamming the opening against the wall. I could have sat on the desk and refused to budge until reinforcements were summoned. The incident shook me up. It was sickening to think that next time I would be smarter.

James got a ten-day suspension but returned in five with the principal's permission. The fake gun incident fast-tracked his evaluation, however. Eight professionals agreed on a diagnosis of behavior disorder. They recommended he go to a special education classroom with about ten children and three adults, where he could work one-on-one to improve his first-grade reading and math skills.

I walked him to his new room and wished him well. I told him that we were his friends and that we would remember him.

I didn't feel bad about James as I had with Pierre, guilty of passing the buck and palming his problems off on another unsuspecting teacher. That is how he came to be with me, but that is not how he left. He left fully evaluated and "serviced." He would get educational services to meet his special needs. His progress would be closely monitored.

"Watch out for your girls," I told his new teacher.

Chapter 38

Dance Africa

Now that I could take children on field trips, I decided that *Dance Africa* would be our first destination. A thrilling spectacle of dance and music, it was staged at the landmark Auditorium Theater downtown. It was an event.

My benefactor agreed to pay for tickets and buses, enough for every child to bring a parent. I thought it would be a wonderful memory for the children, to have a whole day with the undivided attention of their grownups at a fancy show in the city. I was taking my younger daughter, Mia, who was nine, and her friend Sydney. It would be an unusual Saturday afternoon field trip because the show was staged only at night and over the weekend.

The holdup was that the principal had my memo for eight days but claimed no knowledge of my plan every time I asked him. The memo invited him and the vice principal to come along, along with my mentor and Donna and other faculty friends who had helped me out in the past.

I planned to buttonhole him again Monday, but a teacher's mother was laid to rest and few teachers were at school because everyone went to the funeral, an all-day affair.

Also missing in action was one of the second-grade Teachers For Chicago interns. The former insurance agent called it quits after not quite a month. It felt like another death in the family.

But miracle of miracles, later that week we received the go-ahead for our trip, and the permission slips went home. Most of the class was going, and the parents seemed enthusiastic. The kids were in a complete tizzy. I went downtown one day to order the tickets and another day to pick them up. I arranged the buses and acquired the cash to pay the drivers.

All told, the trip cost close to $1,000. My benefactor did not flinch.

While our class counted the days to *Dance Africa* with growing anticipation, I was a nervous wreck. I had never taken seventy people on a trip before. I would cut a Saturday science class at college. There would be hell to pay.

But the experience was a learning one for me. One thing I learned is that if you ever make group reservations for a show, do not tell them you are a public school group. Tell them that you are the Chicago Press Club. Tell them that you are a group of visiting dignitaries from Zimbabwe, coming to see their Iwisi group perform at *Dance Africa* in Chicago.

For if you say that you are a school group, you will sit in the "gallery," a.k.a. the rafters, gasping, listening to your heart palpitate from fear at the dizzying height and feeling that at any second someone is going to pitch forward and plunge, splat, onto the main floor. For this thrill, you will climb six or eight flights of stairs (I lost count) and sputter in disbelief when they tell you that you must go up yet again.

We had a wonderful time.

It was a crisp, sunny fall Saturday as we gathered at the bus. Asophane was the first person I saw when I drove up. She was wearing a beautiful cream-colored party dress with a big bow in the back. She had blue beads in her hair, a cream-colored purse, hose, party shoes and a black leather biker jacket.

I introduced myself to her mother, who quickly scurried off in the opposite direction, "to the store."

Others were waiting, Natasha and her mom, little Minnie with both of her parents, Lucinda with mother and sister, another girl with mom and a brother. I quickly realized that many who signed up were not going to show. We would have many extra tickets, even with the surprise guests. I sent one bus back to the barn, empty.

We still had plenty of room on the one bus for siblings and assorted others. We adopted an "all are welcome" policy, probably breaking various board of education rules.

Two foster children were dropped off by adults who said they could not come along. I took charge of them. We roared off, the Sears Tower looming in the far distance, fifteen miles away. The principal and vice principal were no-shows, but my mentor came along, which was crucial since the other faculty members chose to drive themselves instead of accompany us on the bus.

Roosevelt University is in the same building as the Auditorium Theater, owns it, in fact, and I was able to drop off a pile of unclaimed tickets for my classmates and take my daughter, her friend and the two second graders for a bite to eat in the student lunchroom. My students pointed to focaccia, bananas, and barbecued turkey legs.

"That sure is a big chicken," one observed, carrying a tray with a turkey leg the size of my forearm.

The show was spellbinding, but not to everyone. I told one of my restless charges to memorize all the dance steps, so she could teach the other children on Monday. That kept her busy a while. During the Kenyan dancers, she announced, "This is boring. When are we going home?" I told her to take off her jacket because it was hot. That kept her busy awhile longer.

A couple of the grandmothers looked like they might expire up in the "gallery," so at intermission I asked an usher if we could move down. With his gracious help, I resituated everyone in comfortable seats on the main floor for the second half.

It wasn't until Sweet Honey in the Rock, the Grammy Award-winning a cappella singers, were halfway through their stunningly crafted set that I had a second to enjoy myself. Their rendition of "Motherless Child" was breathtakingly moving. Awakened by one grandmother's shrieks of delight, she being likewise moved, I looked around and saw everyone having a wonderful time. In our cushy new seats, the girls were all sitting together, the boys were all together. Asophane's mother was sitting with one of the dads a few rows down, and Asophane was next to me.

She sat perfectly still, tall atop a pillow made of her jacket and two sweaters. She was intent, a human sponge. She leaned over and whispered, seriously, confidentially, "I really like this."

"I'm glad," I said. "You look like a princess sitting there in your beautiful dress in this beautiful theater."

"I'm going to write about this in my journal on Monday," she whispered, never taking her eyes off the stage.

As her teacher, I savored the moment with all my heart.

My greatest fear was making it back to the bus with the same number of people who got on, but when I counted heads, we were all there.

I heard someone calling my name and saw my neighbor Mike, who is an African drummer, as the bus roared away. We all waved out the windows at him. I told the kids he was leaving for Africa in two weeks and wouldn't come back until March but would come to our class with his cousin next week and play for us. I took pictures of everyone as the bus rolled homeward. As we drew close to school, I announced our next field trip, to the Fire Safety House. Everyone applauded.

As we said our goodbyes outside of school, one grandmother grabbed me in an embrace.

"These children are blessed to have an enthusiastic teacher like you."

It was a wonderful day. It was worth it.

Chapter 39

Loving Louis

One Monday morning, as the children were filing into the classroom, I noticed Louis crumpled in a heap at the bottom of the front wall, holding his hands over his eyes.

"What happened to Louis?" I asked.

"The clock fell off the wall and hit him on the head," I was informed. The suspect clock lay on the floor nearby.

"Speak to me, Louis," I said. "Are you bleeding?"

Silence. Wincing.

I grabbed the ice pack out of my lunch box, wrapped it in a paper towel and had Louis hold it to his wound, a scrape on the bridge of his nose that was not very bloody.

The office was out of Band-Aids, so his cut was evident when he went off with his reading tutor, a retired teacher who volunteered at our school.

"What happened to Louis?" the tutor asked when she brought him back forty minutes later.

"The clock fell off the wall and bonked him on the head," I explained.

She looked at me strangely.

"No," she said. "I meant what happened with his reading. He could read everything today. He did very, very well!"

We looked at each other and burst out laughing.

After she got her breath back she asked, "Do you think you could arrange for the clock to fall on a couple others?"

Louis read that day and one other day. When a teacher's aide came to my room for twenty minutes every morning, I'd sit with a child on the steps outside our classroom and read. Louis and I often worked on *Go, Dog, Go!* One day, he read about half of *Go, Dog, Go!* before he stopped, spent. The exertion left him sweaty, and when he went back into the room, he needed a nap on the rug. He tried his best for me, but reading was beyond his grasp all but those two days.

His other tutors quit on him, because he would crawl on the floor and goof around instead of getting with the program. I offered to tutor him outside school hours, but his parents didn't respond to my phone calls or notes home. I figured there was a lot going on there, because he told hair-raising stories sometimes.

"Two men busted into our house when me and my brother was watching TV last night. We told them our mother wasn't selling crack anymore, but they took our TV anyway…"

I loved Louis because with all the impossible shit he had stacked against him, he had the kindest heart. He didn't turn mean or spiteful or shut himself off from the world. He just kept on being Louis.

He had no hang-ups. When a friend suggested to him that "Mrs. B. was white," he replied, "No, man, Mrs. B. ain't white, she's light-skinned." He never thought twice about putting on pink satin pointe shoes. If he was interested, he dove right in, and so to me, he was a joy. I loved his gravelly voice, I loved the way he showed off his muscles, but had a gentle way with other children. Yes, he would swing on the bathroom door frames and hide in the coatroom and frustrate me with his endless wandering about the room and racing in the lunchroom, but I loved him completely. Maybe it was because of the Beatles, who said "all you need is love."

I'm a big Beatles fan, always have been, and I like to think that I spread some of their magic around the second grade. We did ballet to Otis Redding and mastered all twelve verses of "Over in the Meadow" (and God knows the Rolling Stones sustained me more than anything else), but in second grade, we listened the most to the Beatles.

The winter of second grade the Beatles had both the best-selling book and top album in the world. Louis, my multiple intelligence learner, came in one morning to report that he had seen the Beatles on a new TV at home the night before.

"What were they doing?" I asked. Louis slid down on his knees and played air guitar.

"They were playing 'Yellow Submarine'," he said. "And you know what, Mrs. B.?"

He looked up at me like the cat that swallowed the canary.

"They broke up!"

"What!" I said, grabbing my head. "The Beatles broke up? Oh no!"

"What?" cried the other children.

"The Beatles broke up!"

"Oh no!" they said, grabbing their heads.

At lunch I filled Louis in. I told him the Fab Four called it quits thirty years ago, when I was in high school and his mother wasn't even born.

"But isn't it amazing," I said, "that the music they made back then still matters to us today?"

"Yeah," he said. "I love the Beatles."

Louis still couldn't read. But he had gotten deep into some words in our classroom. In the listening lab, when I thought he was reading along to *Pecos Bill*, he was listening to *Abbey Road*. He had secretly switched the tapes. I put two and two together one day when I noticed him singing softly to himself while he was coloring.

"Mean Mr. Mustard sleeps in the park, shaves in the dark..." Louis' song faded out as he colored a little more. "Such a mean old man," he started up singing again. "Such a mean old man!" he sang with gusto, coloring furiously.

Louis took information from our classroom, connected it to something out in the world and reported back to us. He came to school ready to teach me a thing or two, and that's pretty good for a seven-year-old.

I was figuring out other ways to turn their needs into learning experiences.

Daily, they'd come to me when they had a stomachache or a loose tooth, and they expected me do to something about it. I cannot bear to pull teeth and my ink-stained, broken down overstuffed chair (a.k.a. the "sick bay") had long ago gone out into the dumpster. But Trey said he knew how to pull teeth, and that is how he became our official dentist. If you had a loose tooth, you were sent to Trey with a couple of tissues.

We started a doctor's office in our classroom. The kids had to write down the names of their patients, their complaints, read first-aid procedures and measure blood pressure and temperature. It was so popular, I had to buy more supplies and expand it into a hospital. We went through Band-Aids, gauze and tape like the Battle of Gettysburg. One day, I thought I caught some people fooling around. They were lying on the floor.

"What's going on here?" I asked.

"Rico is having surgery!"

"Asophane is having a baby!"

"Good heavens!" I said. "At the same time? In the same operating room?"

"Yes," replied the fevered team of doctors, as one, not looking up from their work.

"Carry on!" I barked as I went to check the next wing, where broken arms and legs were being wrapped in yet more gauze.

Most days left me shell-shocked. The incessant questions! "Mrs. B.! Mrs. B.!" a thousand times a day. The patting when they wanted your attention, your arm, your shoulder, your hand, your back. Every day, "ketchup hands" on my shirt.

But in the midst of it all, we managed to find our pace, our groove, and I would not trade anything for those moments of grace when the learning spell charms everyone, when every kid is civil and focused and trying their best.

They come every so often. One Friday afternoon, we pulled out our watercolor sets. We had learned the colors of the rainbow, we had seen how prisms split white light into colors. Now it was time to mix some colors. We mixed blue and red and made purple. We mixed red and yellow and made orange. We mixed blue and yellow and made green. That was all I knew, so that was a good time to pass out paper and brushes and let the painting settle into a quiet rhythm of its own.

"Can we listen to some music?" someone asked.

"Sure," I said, thinking I'd tune in the classical station.

"Put on the Beatles!" the class shouted.

"It would be my pleasure," I replied.

There they all were, painting in the afternoon sun, singing "We All Live in a Yellow Submarine."

In that moment, we lived the life of ease. Every one of us had all we needed. Sky of blue and sea of green were being brushed on white paper. Our friends were all aboard.

Chapter 40

The Downside

I informed my parents, sadly, that I couldn't come for Thanksgiving. I was too tired. All the interns were exhausted. We had eye infections. We were surly. We were not amused. We were stressed from poverty. I tallied up my school expenses and found I'd spent more than $2,000 on classroom supplies and college textbooks in the year 2000. My reimbursement was $100.

The butt of our wrath at the moment was our science methods teacher, who did not seem to fully grasp that we were classroom teachers working daily in impossible conditions. When she returned all of our homework to us one Saturday, I noticed that we all got the same grade on every paper. That grade and nothing else. I flipped through the pages looking for comments or feedback, and seeing none, asked her why.

"I just didn't have time," she said. "If I did that, I'd still be grading them."

We looked at her dumbfounded. We, who include a mother of two young children and the wife of a cop, who regularly gets up at 3:30 a.m. when her house is quiet to work on her college homework. We, who bothered to do her stupid Internet search assignment, even though we had just done the same thing in a more complicated way in our technology class the summer before. We, who teach all day every day, grade our students' papers and return them with comments and feedback.

Nice modeling for teachers. She earned $1,800 for teaching five sessions, three of which ended hours early. It took us twelve days to earn that much money. We never got out early. When we graded our students' papers, we looked at their work. We did not give everyone the same grade.

While the whole group of interns was exhausted, as the oldest I may have been feeling it more than the others. And the fatigue was not just physical. It was mental as well. I was drained more every day by the limits of poverty, by the racism, the unprofessional manner in which our school was run, the criticism, the nit-picking, the zero encouragement or respect. No one ever told you when you did a good job. It was like no other job situation I had ever experienced.

Despite promises to come to each intern's room for an hour each day, our mentor had not been present. She helped me rearrange my students' desks one day. The intern across the hall adopted the veteran second-grade teacher as her mentor, which was very wise.

We confronted the academic fraud of "Walking Reading," in which the children are grouped by ability and marched to another room for reading first thing in the morning. We gritted our teeth and endured it because it looked good on paper. Our schedules made it impossible most days. When we did it, it was disruptive. The children hated it. Martin cried every time.

"I want to stay here with you," he'd plead. When he started hiding in the coatroom, I relented and let him stay. He was relieved and happy.

We administered tests on a quarterly basis, tests abandoned by the board years ago. We didn't have enough instruction manuals because they were out of print. Yet there was no talk of a more modern or authentic testing method. Just do it, get the results in quarterly and don't make waves was the message. It was just something someone could point to on paper that we did.

I had received $900 worth of books for my classroom through a grant, plus about four days of intense instruction in teaching reading over the summer. So my reading program was the most effected because we didn't work out of textbooks known as basal readers.

The whole "under my thumb" vibe prevented any sort of protest, and without a free flow of ideas and opinions, mistrust flourished. I noticed that the office ladies in the other building, who worked along-side me the year before, stopped saying hello unless I spoke first. I won-dered why.

There was talk of "looping"—following your students from year to year. People seemed to assume I'd stay after my internship was up. They talked about me following my second graders into third grade.

But I was tired of it all. I needed to find a place where I was not "one of the white teachers" or a pretender or a problem. I had to find a more supportive school where I was viewed as competent and dedicated. I was curious to see how the principal would handle it at year's end. Would he ask me to stay? I rather doubted it.

There had been no mention of resolving my "remediation," which was up at the quarter, according to terms on the table the previous year. I decided to simply wait it out and see what would happen. Still, it was a constant, nagging worry to me. I wondered whether the unre-solved documents were in a personnel file somewhere. In the end, no one ever brought it up again. Not once.

A new layer of stress was introduced when Martin was absent a whole week. I asked the kids if they'd seen him.

"Martin's gone, Mrs. Baldacci. His house is abandoned," Andrea told me.

My heart sank. I had visions of Kayla's disappearance, which still grieved me. The thought of losing Martin was too much to think about that grim fall.

I decided to wait until Monday to report his extended absence to the office. Maybe he has chicken pox, I told myself. That's good for a week.

To my great relief and joy, he walked through the door on Monday, scrubbed and in a stiff new white shirt. I hugged him tight and asked him where he had been.

"My house burned down," he said softly. I noticed he didn't have his book bag, just a plastic grocery bag. He apologized, sadly, because *Tiki Tiki Tembo*, the book he borrowed from the class library, along with his book bag, was in the boarded-up, burned-out house.

"Don't worry about that one bit," I told him. "You are safe, and your family is safe and that's all that matters. I don't know what we'd do if anything happened to you."

He carried bus tickets and was late every day. He must have been staying far from school.

The year before, one of my college classmates' first graders was killed in a fire. She didn't ever talk about it. Teachers keep a lot of things bottled up inside.

Chapter 41

Another Christmas

The second week in December, my car got "booted" in the school parking lot. Two three-year-old parking tickets had come back to haunt me. I was caught in a city collection crackdown that targeted municipal employees. The month before, bus drivers with unpaid tickets got the boot at their workplace parking lots. School employees were next in the crosshairs. Without warning, I was called to the principal's office.

"Is this your license plate number?" the principal asked me, handing me a piece of paper.

"Yes, why?" I asked. No answer.

"What's going on?" I asked.

"Why don't you go take a look at your car?" he said.

"What happened? Did a dumpster fall on it?" I asked. Getting a big insurance check for my old car would not be such a terrible thing. The suspense was killing me, but the principal wouldn't talk, so I dashed outside without my coat to find the big yellow vice on my front wheel. Several other teachers' cars were in the same pinch.

I got a ride home from Astrid, and then my neighbor, Andre, drove me to the payment center fifteen minutes away. In line was the calm first-grade intern with her father, who was bailing her out. We were sort of mortified, but the line was long with scofflaws who were paying fines to the same mayor who signed their paychecks.

"Come on, we all work for the city. Can't we work something out?" one man pleaded, trying to bargain with the agent behind the window. No deals were made. I got the boot off by charging $500 on Visa.

When the second graders asked, "Do you give Christmas presents, Mrs. Baldacci?" I could only groan.

I had planned to give every child a class picture for Christmas. Only two kids had purchased a class picture after "Ol' Mr. One Shot" had posed us in the school library one morning in the fall. I called him that because both years, he shot our class pictures in one take. It amazed me that he could get thirty-six people in synch and the lighting right in a single shot. When I saw the results, of course, it was apparent he was not a genius of photography, but a cheapskate in a hurry. In our second-grade class picture, we looked more spiffy than in seventh, when we posed on the auditorium stage. But there were junky magazine racks and other mess in the background and around the edges that made it look cheesy.

At any rate, I figured I could crop it and print it at home using the computer and give each child a copy for Christmas at a cost of less than $100. Which was still money I didn't have. As I was fretting over the Denver Boot and my perilous finances, a friend called and said her church did something every year for an "underprivileged" family and figured I knew one I could recommend.

"Instead of one family, could you do something for thirty-two children?" I asked her.

The result was that every kid in the class would receive a doll and a book, or a Hot Wheels kit and a book. It was so unexpected, so fantastic, I didn't realize until later how sexist our choices were. I should have asked for doctor kits all around.

Earlier in December, we observed the anniversary of John Lennon's death by watching *A Hard Day's Night*. Practically every child in the class had a brush with gun violence. They had lost relatives or friends, had escaped gunfire or heard it in the neighborhood and knew to get down. When they were first graders, the gun drama at our school the year before had taken place practically under their noses. One of my girls, a prolific writer who loved the blue marble composition notebook I'd provided for reading/writing workshop, had written about a friend who was killed.

"On my weekend I road my bike me and my sister. We went a round the block. Then it was gun shots. When the gun shots where done my mom said come in."

Not everyone escaped unscathed that night, I gathered, for the next page was dedicated "For Nesha, She was my best friend. I wish she was alive."

Underneath was a picture of a lightning bolt colored blue and orange and red, which is how gunfire looks at night coming out of the barrel of a gun. Under the lightning bolt was a small girl with tears dripping down her cheeks, asking "Why?"

Later, that same child would write in her journal about leaving school early on a May afternoon to visit a friend in the hospital.

"I was so happy I mean so happy she got shot in her leg. But she will be OK. She might live with me one day."

During *A Hard Day's Night*, the children kept asking when the part was coming where John gets killed.

We stopped the movie and made a Beatles timeline on the board. When they saw that the movie was about a different place and time, happy and simple, they were vastly relieved. We put the movie back on and jitterbugged to "Can't Buy Me Love." The newest Beatle fans were Tashequa, Mario and Enrico, who we nicknamed Ringo. Tashequa pulled me aside during the movie and explained that she didn't want any boyfriends because she got raped when she was six. I hugged her and told her how sorry I was that happened to her, that it happens to a lot of girls, and that it wasn't her fault. Talking about gun violence stirred up other memories of violence. She said the man who hurt her was in prison just like the man who killed John.

I did not breathe a word about Christmas. When the children arrived for the last day of school before Christmas break, a half-day, there was great suspense about the large, mysterious black bags stacked in the corner. I said I had no idea what they were, that they'd just been there when I came in that morning, but maybe we'd have time to look inside after our lesson.

After a read-aloud of *The Grinch Who Stole Christmas* and a bathroom break, we dragged the bags onto the blue rug and spilled out a treasure trove of beautifully gift-wrapped presents. We made a boy pile and a girl pile of the big boxes, then a third pile of the smaller, thin gifts. The children figured out instantly by the shape and hardness that those packages contained books. Two at a time, a boy and a girl went up and made their choices: one box, one book. It took a long time for some people to choose. I watched them with one box in each hand, weighing their choice: "Do I want the beautiful gold wrapping paper or the box that isn't as pretty, but is bigger?" When everyone had drawn from the pile, we unwrapped together. Such excitement—flying paper and ribbons, jumping up and down, a frenzy of joy! The best part: Everyone got exactly what they wanted. There was no "I like yours better." There was only, "Look what I got!" Each thought their own was best. The Hot Wheels cars were all complete kits, cars with garages and police stations and car washes. The baby dolls were exquisite. No two were the same. We oohed and aahed like relatives outside a hospital nursery. The dolls went home snuggled inside the coats of their new mothers. If you were wondering, they were all babies in beautiful shades of brown. The boys made plans to get together over the holidays to build huge cities out of their car sets.

After the children left, there was a Christmas luncheon for the teachers in the library. I was antsy, because ten of my children had not come to school on that bitterly cold half-day. Like Santa, I had deliveries to make.

I peeled out of the parking lot at 2:18, twelve minutes early. First stop was Natasha's grandmother's house. All her brothers, sisters and cousins were there.

"It was just too cold to send them to school for a half-day," grandma explained. I agreed. I met Natasha's grandfather and his brother as the other children ran to the back of the house hollering for Natasha to come quick.

The shy, tiniest fairy came down the long hallway with a quizzical look on her face. When she saw me standing in her grandmother's living room, she bolted into a run and jumped into my arms, a huge smile on her face. I spun her around and told her we'd missed her at the party.

"I've come to ask you something," I told her. "If you were picked to be the mother of a special baby doll, would you want a great big one or a tiny little one like you?"

"A great big one," she said. "The biggest."

"Wait here," I told her. I went to my car trunk and took out the biggest box. She unwrapped it on the spot. It was a beautiful baby with a blue fuzzy sleeper and a stocking cap. "Thank heavens that baby has warm clothes for a day like this," I observed. The book she unwrapped was *Green Eggs and Ham*, her favorite. Grandma hugged me goodbye and blessed me as I set off into the biting cold.

Next stop was Mario's. He was in his undershirt. His mother made him put his boxes under the tree until Christmas. On my way once again, I turned a corner where three boys playing in the snow paused and shouted out, "Mrs. Baldacci! Mrs. Baldacci!"

I couldn't tell who they were because they were so bundled up, but I stopped, waved and told them "Merry Christmas!" It had been more than thirty years, back when my husband was a child, since any kids shouted "Mrs. Baldacci!" on the streets of Roseland.

Next stop was a second-floor apartment above a storefront, up a steep staircase to a cozy den. "Tell your teacher thank you and give her a hug," Tashequa's mother told her, smiling over her daughter's head at me.

Hakim was wearing pajamas and a twinkling smile.

"Put them under the tree," said his beautiful mother.

"If that book is too easy for you, you can swap when we get back to school," I told him.

One more delivery, to a girl in pajamas whose sister got her nose out of joint when she saw the gift-wrapped box. A condemnation notice was nailed to the doorframe. That was my last delivery, but one present remained in my trunk, a baby doll for a girl with no address. She would have to wait until school resumed, assuming she came back then.

It was dark as I headed home from my rounds. Christmas lights twinkled in the neighborhood; the all-blue display was popular that year. Trees glowed behind living room windows.

I tuned in the classical station and thought about the day. Far more had come out of those big black bags than surprisingly wonderful toys. The church people who wanted to help had put something in motion that would last long after the toys were cast aside and the books were memorized by heart. They had reinforced the image of our school and classroom as places where good and fun things happen, where people care about each other, where magic occasionally breaks out, where rewards are bestowed and love abounds. For children who learned young that life was uncertain and often cruel, and that institutions were not to be trusted, that was the most important gift of all.

Chapter 42

Cruel January

The first week back from the long Christmas break was brutal, like a week full of Mondays.

The kids, predictably, had a hard time getting back with the program. Our time away from school had been blissfully unstructured. By Friday my head was ringing with the incessant drone of "Mrs. Baldacci, Mrs. Baldacci, Mrs. Baldacci, Mrs. Baldacci, Mrs. Baldacci, Mrs. Baldacci, Mrs. Baldacci." They were happy to see me, I supposed.

Asophane was behaving like a short timer and told me she was transferring out of our school. I called her mother, who said she had no intention of transferring her. She came back the next day as her old hard-working self.

Brandon was angry and refusing to work. I made him line leader and he rose to the challenge. By week's end (and two phone calls home) he was on board.

Louis was crawling on the floor again. I phoned his home from the classroom cell phone and put him on with his mother. It reduced him to tears but got him back in his seat, albeit upside-down.

The biggest surprise was Enrico. He was back on the job. Didn't fight with anyone. He did not make faces or talk back. I called his mother to report this change. She informed me she had gotten married over the holiday, and they had moved. "He now has a positive male role model in his life," she said. "It's making all the difference."

They hadn't forgotten how to read. Everyone was eager to get a book out of the library. Three asked me to read to the class the books they'd gotten for Christmas, claiming that no one had read with them at home over the holiday, and they did not take it upon themselves to crack the new books. I thought the truth was that they wanted to show off their books to the class, which was good. It demonstrated that they were proud of their books and wanted to share them.

Reading about Dr. King in preparation for the January 15 holiday, there was a passage in one book about how Martin, as a boy, would spend all his allowance on books because he wanted to own his own books. Everyone's head snapped up at that part. Something resonated. They all had their own books. They were impressed that he graduated from high school and started college at age fifteen.

"See where reading can take you?" I said.

There was an open house at a new, all-girl charter school on Sunday afternoon. At the start-up, they were only taking girls in sixth and ninth grades. I planned to take Mia for a look-see, and told some of my former seventh graders, now eighth graders, about it. They came hunting me the next day and asked me to take them, which is probably a violation of the Mann Act or ten different teacher rules. They always warn teachers to never take a student in their cars, never be alone with a student, especially with the classroom door closed. You never know what someone will say about you.

On Sunday, it was freezing cold. Mia had a fever. I called Nichelle to tell her I didn't think I'd be able to take them without a chaperone. Her mother couldn't come. She worked nights and needed her rest. Destinee's granddad wasn't feeling too good and he begged off. Kyisha's mother was home with the twins, who had just turned one.

Hearing the disappointment in Nichelle's voice, I decided to take them anyway. I knocked on each door and personally took the hand-off from each grown-up, along with signed notes from each adult saying it was okay for the girls to go with me. Off we went to the school, which was on the Illinois Institute of Technology campus near Comiskey Park.

"Put on your seat belts," I told each one as we roared off. They admired my Dodge Neon's upholstery.

They were perfectly behaved, delightful. We looked all around, talked to students, met the principal and went to every classroom. We attracted a few quizzical looks, these three beautiful black teenage girls and one short light-skinned woman. One teacher asked them if their parents were there, and they said they came with me, their old teacher. "You must be pretty special students," she said, smiling. I agreed that yes, they definitely were.

They were some of the same girls who had been present at the crying-in-the-bathroom incident more than a year before. So of course we checked out the bathroom facilities at the new school. Gleaming new tile. Many, many bathroom stalls, each with a door that closed and locked. Hot and cold running water. Soap. Mirrors, lots of them, reflected our faces. We were all smiling. Smiling at how far we had come. They were about to graduate grammar school. I would finish graduate school in June. I like to think we kept each other going.

As far as I know, they all sent in their applications. It would be a great environment: fifteen girls in a class. The only all-girl public school. The thing that impressed me the most about that charter school was that they didn't give letter grades. Projects were graded on a level of mastery: complete, in progress and "not yet." Every project was graded on a rubric of about twenty items that must be completed, and how well each detail was presented.

I felt like such a fraud giving letter grades on the report cards of my students that weekend. How can you give a seven-year-old an F because he can't read? Louis felt bad about his grades, and I spent special time with him alone on Friday to show him the progress he had made since the start of the year.

"Look, Louis, now all your people have hair and hands and shoes. And you are making animals and houses now. My favorite pictures are you doing *grand jeté*. And look what you did last week—you added a sentence to your drawing. You are coming along. Keep working hard. I will help you."

He was so happy to hear this that he drew a picture for me. He asked my favorite color, the girls' favorite colors and Artie's favorite color.

"This is you, your daughters and your husband, and the cats, Midnight and Sam," he said. Every one of us was drawn in our favorite color. He got every one right. Is it any wonder I adored Louis?

He had drawn a picture of me with Midnight the week before. Midnight had a turned-down cat mouth.

"Is Midnight sad?" I asked.

"You are at school and he misses you," Louis replied.

I gave the picture to Mia, since Midnight is her cat. I asked her could she write a note to Louis. She wrote:

"Dear Louis,

"I really like the picture you drew of my mom and Midnight. I don't think he's sad when we are away because he always finds some crazy thing to do to amuse himself. Did you know that we have another cat, Sam? So Midnight has someone to play with when we are gone, and he is never bored.

Write back!"

Mia was home sick from school that week, and I phoned her after lunch from the classroom. It was very quiet, as it is whenever I pull out the phone, because someone's usually getting a phone call home and everyone wants to hear them get in trouble.

"How are you feeling?" I asked. She said she was okay, she guessed. I asked her if she'd say hi to Louis, and passed the phone.

"Someone wants to talk to you," I told him.

"Hello," he said. "Hi, Mia." Big, big smile. Quiet. "I got your letter," he said softly.

They didn't have too much to say, but Mia told him to write her back, and he said he would.

After he hung up, I said, "Hey, why don't we all write to her? When you're home sick, wouldn't you feel better if someone sent you a get-well note?"

Paper and pencils at the ready, we brainstormed.

I hope you are feeling better.

I hope you get well.

I hope you get better so you can come visit our classroom.

I hope you get better so you can come on our field trip with us.

I hope you get better soon so you can go back to school and learn something.

Mia had eighteen get-well notes that night, some in homemade envelopes sealed with spit. They made her feel much better. It made me feel great. It is the essence of writing to communicate feelings to another person with pencil and paper and, yes, spit. They are getting quite good at it. Some of the boys put: "Look on back."

We turned over their letters and found that they'd provided their phone numbers.

There were a few totally original letters in the mix.

"I'm sorry you are sick. I am sick, too."

"Remember me from the *Dance Africa* field trip? I hope you feel better."

Mia wasn't the only one who was sick. I had some horrid virus with a disgusting cough and much nose-blowing and sneezing. My hearing went in and out. Everything that could be infected was, even an earring hole.

I rested all weekend and prayed for a snow day Monday. Freezing rain was predicted. The streets and sanitation department put down tons of road salt, and school was on as usual.

But not for long. A power outage at school caused us to evacuate.

We lined up in the darkened hallways and boarded buses to South Side Prep for the day. It was Artie's former Catholic boys' high school, and we spent the day in the gym not doing much of anything. We sang "Down By the Bay" about a thousand times. We tried to read a few books, but it was so noisy I just had them read to themselves. We went to the bathroom and for drinks of water a dozen times. We had a very good lunch! We returned to school forty minutes late, all of us wrung out and exhausted. Their homework was to write a story about "My Crazy Day." Only Mario did his homework.

We noodled around the next day. We had library. We worked with math manipulatives on subtraction regrouping. We watched the dance scenes from a ballet movie called *Center Stage*. They got to see men and women at ballet, an African-American prima ballerina in *Swan Lake*, the balcony scene from *Romeo and Juliet* and a *pas de quatre* from *Swan Lake*, a rocking jazz class and ballet classes at American Ballet

Theater Academy. It was very exciting and got everyone spinning and walking on tiptoes.

My homeless girl was spending her days sitting under a table or in a corner in the afternoons, frustrated beyond all comprehension. The situation was urgent. My request for referral forms was ten days unanswered.

Later that week, we took our field trip to the Fire Safety House. Afterward, we shared and everyone showed their burn scars. We had several scars from hot irons, a hot pan spilling off the stove, a burn from an exhaust pipe on a motorcycle and assorted curling irons on the neck. Ouch.

I did not turn in my lesson plans on Friday. They were not done. I was a total wreck. I was crying Thursday night because of various roadblocks to getting my second-year book grant application turned in. The line at the one working copy machine in the Roosevelt library included seven people with thick books.

Saturday I went to the doctor. The nurse asked, "Are you running a fever?"

"I don't know. We broke the thermometer."

She took my temp. It was 100.

"You have a fever," she said.

"That explains the otherworldly feeling I've been having," I said.

The doctor looked in my eyes, ears, throat. He listened to me breathe. He said, "I'm going to give you a shot. Then you will take Zithromax for a week. If you don't feel better, you have a refill. Take it another week."

"What do I have?" I ask.

"A little of this, a little of that," he says. I figured as much. Earache, cough, nose-blowing like there's no tomorrow, big fatigue.

"What have you been doing for it?" he asked.

"Nothing. Being a jerk. Going to work every day. Oh, I found some Amoxicillin in the cupboard and took it for three days when my chest started to hurt from coughing."

"How old was it?" he asked.

"Expired a year ago July," I said. "I stole it from my husband."

The nurse came back to give me my shot, and I started to drop my pants.

"No!" she cried. "We only do that with little kids. By the time you're a grown-up, you have enough meat on your arms to take a shot up there."

"Oh," I said. I hadn't had a shot for being sick since I was a little kid.

Monday at school I had Brandon dress up like the doctor and Andrea as me. We rolled out a new feature, "401 Theater." We acted out my episode at the doctor's office. I showed them where I got my shot. Everyone applauded.

We had many volunteers who wanted to act out scenes from their lives. The point: There are many ways to tell a story. I was feeling a bit better by the way.

The children worked magnificently. They took a reading review quiz of our read-alouds from the week, four questions on each story.

They did their fire safety quiz. We colored a while. I noticed some children chose sheets with cats in a garden, others picked lions in a jungle. We did a compare and contrast on lions and cats with a Venn diagram. I thought I'd pass out before they finally came up with the words "wild" and "tame."

We had lunch and gym, and then we watched *The Dancing Princesses* from Shelley Duvall's Fairy Tale Theatre. The next day we would read *Brothers of the Knight*, about Reverend Knight and his twelve sons in Harlem. The children would see how fairy tales have eternal themes and how stories morph and time travel, in print, on the stage and in film. We were back in the groove.

Chapter 43

A Prayer in School

I had been weary. Beaten down. It was that "Slipping Into Darkness" time of year again in Chicago, a time of short days and icy winds and ankle-deep gray slush at every corner. It was hard to get motivated. I was overdue for a moment of grace.

As I was warming up the room by positioning our fan to pull warm air from the hallway, the office called to say that a parent had come to see me. I went downstairs and found Tashiqua with her grandfather.

We went upstairs and sat in the yellow chairs at the small desks. He said Tashiqua had been troubled by people "talking about her mama" the day before. I recalled a spat between Tashiqua and another girl at her table. Tashiqua had asked to move her desk across the room, and I had allowed it.

Her granddad said that Tashiqua was a compassionate person and that he believed from a prophecy that she would be a great and holy woman. I agreed. I told him what a delight she was and how I loved having such a special person in my class.

I explained that everyone comes through our door with baggage, with issues. I said I wanted our room to be a compassionate community, supportive of each other. I admitted it was a struggle.

Just then, Andrea walked in. It was ten minutes too early, and she knew she was to line up outside with the class, but she blurted out that she was absent the day before because her cousin died and she was at her funeral.

Everything stopped. Andrea handed me the funeral program she carried in her hand. I told her how sorry I was. I asked her about her cousin, how she died, had she been sick, how old was she, and finally, how she herself was doing.

Tashiqua's grandfather, who I rightly assumed was a pastor, then asked her would she like to pray on it for a moment? Andrea went right to him. We all bowed our heads. He prayed beautifully, soothing words of comfort and hope. I thought of Kayla.

Afterward, I told Andrea she could put her cousin's program up on the board for the day if she'd like, and she did. Even when someone is gone, we remember them.

Tashiqua and her granddad and I talked a while longer about how we have to meet insult with love. I talked about how we each bear crosses. Granddad smiled and said he had uttered those exact words that morning.

I thanked him for his prayer and for supporting Andrea. I felt, too, the healing power of prayer in my public school classroom. I had a calm and centered day.

Not long after that, I learned that Kayla was alive and well! The guidance counselor told me the news. She was enrolled at another school in the neighborhood in eighth grade. She didn't lose any ground in her year away.

I asked whether it would be appropriate to try to contact her. I wondered if I could write a letter of recommendation for her for high school. The guidance counselor said she would let me know.

The job of teaching, performed with an open heart, carries a burden of grief. I could not dwell on Kayla, in thought or conversation, without becoming teary. I'd slap myself for being such a baby. I'd tell myself to snap out of it, no one died, for crying out loud. I told myself that bad things happen to good people and that kids bounce back. But still I grieved.

For a year I had lit candles. I had worried and wondered whether I would ever see her again and how it would happen. In one of my sappy daydreams I imagined myself as an old lady teacher meeting a student teacher, a young woman wearing a gold medal of *La Madonna della Strada*.

The sadness I carried for an entire year, the shock at her disappearance, not knowing where she was or if she was all right, at last lifted. I was overjoyed!

Knowing she was back was not enough, though. I wanted to know how she was doing. I wondered if she might be interested in that Young Women's Leadership Charter School and whether I could help her get in.

Over the next weeks, I phoned the guidance counselor of her new school a number of times. The counselor was always "not here yet" or "just left." I finally caught her in the early afternoon one day and explained the situation. I asked if she could tell Kayla I wanted to see her, and if it was okay with Kayla's mother, set up a meeting.

The counselor agreed. I never got a call back, however. My subsequent calls were not returned.

I tried Kayla's pastor and her aunt with the same results.

Finally, I just had to let it go.

Chapter 44

Recess!

There were four days until March, and we started putting our weather time line up. Hakim drew some of his fantastic, fierce lions for our calendar board and we put up the words: "March comes in like a lion."

I had written a memo asking that the class be allowed to go on a walk around the block every day to observe the changing season for our weather unit. We would make scientific notations of the daily changes. In Chicago, March is a monumental month of nature's fury and affirmation.

I got my memo back from the office secretary.

"He said to tell you that if you send a memo, you should send it to him and 'cc' the others," she said. The memo was addressed to my mentor, the vice principal and the principal, in that order.

"Did he say anything about the content of the memo itself?" I asked.

"No," she said.

"So I should resubmit it with his name first and 'cc' the ladies?" I asked.

She nodded her head.

We never did get permission for our daily walks. The reason given was safety.

"I don't want my name in the paper if something happens to those children out there," said the vice principal.

"Out there" was our neighborhood. How could we, as adults responsible for the well-being of children, be fearful of our neighborhood? What kind of message did that send to the children? What kind of line did that draw?

On the rare occasions that teachers needed to stay until 6 p.m. for report card pickup, they were urged to go out to their cars in groups, reinforcing the perception of the neighborhood as a dangerous, high-crime area. Every day at 2:30, most teachers fled the building like a fire drill. Yet our students walked to and from school, most without adult supervision.

I did not have the fortitude to dig my heels in for a "take back the neighborhood" initiative in which the school leadership had no interest. But philosophically I found it sad that the staff was afraid of the neighborhood, as sad as the principal believing that the students were "victims." It showed a lack of faith and encouraged the mindset of excuse-making. It probably had a lot to do with low achievement. I gave up the idea of outdoor science walks.

But I got a new idea from our "Math Mania" day. Math Mania was a circus of math-connected activities in the classroom: Crazy Eights and Old Maid card games; jacks; building blocks and tessellations, which are repeating designs with colorful geometric shapes. Everyone seemed to find an activity they were interested in. The children followed their interests and formed small groups. The groups changed as students became bored with one activity and tried another. No one tormented anyone. No one fought. No one used the free time to go in someone else's desk or coat pockets. Everyone was busy. No one acted stressed out or negative.

It slowly dawned on me that we needed to do this every day and call it indoor recess. Given the stress levels of the children, with no physical release except gym once a week, the kids needed to play. And since they tended to fuss and fight at the silliest provocation, the children needed to learn to play together.

Cleaning out the basement, I found a hopscotch rug that had belonged to my daughters. I brought it to school with four rocks to use as markers. The first time we tried it invited chaos. Everyone crowded in, butted in line and fought over taking turns.

But when we opened up other activities in the room, we created an indoor playground. Four people at a time played hopscotch while others played ball or jacks on the floor. Someone brought out a jump rope and we moved desks to make room for that. Others gravitated to our popular "doctor's office" for role-playing with dolls.

The children created their own mix of aerobic exercise and simple stress-relieving imaginative play. The next day, we tried it again. Before long, the set-up and clean-up were much quicker, the transitions easier, and groups were cooperating better than before. Children who did not wish to play went next door to read to the kindergartners, another positive example of cooperation.

I was there if they needed me to show how to deal cards, but they were in charge of themselves. They chose their games and their playmates.

As time went on, I observed the children's activities during our secret recess and the mood of the classroom afterward. Cooperative and imaginative play continued to improve.

I was worried that I'd get in trouble. I figured it was a matter of time before I had to do a tap dance justifying our playtime. I choreographed one that extolled the math skills, especially when we made a store with empty food boxes and a cash register out of a kitchen drawer organizer. Louis was exceptional at counting change.

All of the fun and games were my best efforts to make our classroom a place where "a splendid time was guaranteed for all."

Chapter 45

The Teacher Certification Test

If questions on the Basic Skills Test for teachers two years before had been like the under-$8,000 questions on *Who Wants to Be a Millionaire?* the state certification test was more like *Jeopardy*. We needed to know our teacher stuff and a whole lot more.

It was a glorious summer-like April day, a far cry from the freezing, snow-covered day that I took the Basic Skills Test in what seemed like another lifetime. The test was at the same place, a high school on the city's southwest side. Hundreds of seagulls circled the green sports fields. My fellow interns clustered on the steps, nervous, giving each other pep talks.

We had not prepared other than to give ourselves the self-test at the back of the state board of education book, which was quite detailed and explained every answer, right and wrong. I reviewed it twice.

Some people spend weeks or months preparing for the test. They join study groups at their colleges of education or send to the state board of education for additional prep materials.

But my colleagues and I had no time for that. We were in the waning days of our internship. One more report card and we were out. Our days as classroom intern teachers were coming to an end and so were our nights at graduate school. After living and breathing education day and night, I felt we were perfectly positioned to ace the test.

Again, it was a multiple choice test. It was like Trivial Pursuit with chart and map reading. "Who was the president of the Confederacy during the Civil War?" "What African country is shown on the map?" There were diagrams and trick questions. My favorite: "If you were paving a parking lot with a two-inch-thick coat of asphalt, how many cubic feet of material would you need?" There were questions about which activities are most appropriate for children of different ages, questions about first aid and team sports, questions about behaviorist theory, how kids learn and how to best handle misbehavers.

The undergraduate biology lab I had taken the fall before at a Chicago community college served me well in the science area. Again, I did poorest in language arts—after supporting myself as a writer for twenty-five years!

The results: Language Arts, 93. Mathematics and Science, 96. Social Studies, 100. Health, Physical Education and Fine Arts, 100. Professional Knowledge, 100. Total score: 97. We needed a 70 to pass. Some of my colleagues failed, and some failed for the second time.

Were those who failed poor teachers? Not from what I had seen. I had worked on projects, presentations and lesson plans with them, and their work was thoughtful, creative, solid and mindful of "best practice." Their students did well. In my opinion, their test results didn't reflect their knowledge or talent. I did not know what to make of it. Were they nervous, knowing the career for which they'd prepared for two years was on the line? Did they read too much into the questions or read them incorrectly? It made no sense.

The experience made me sympathize with my own students, who live and die by their Iowa test scores. It confirmed my skepticism about what standardized tests really measure as far as what we know and how we apply that knowledge.

I realized:

- How well, how much and what we read greatly influences how well we do on tests.
- Despite our frenzy to ignite critical thinking in our students, it is deadly to "over-think" a question on a standardized test.
- It is better to stick to a basic formula than to write with passion, style or voice.
- It is possible to score 100s across the board on the teacher test yet lack the creativity, humanity and stamina it takes to be a teacher in this day and age.

After the test, Tammy and Michelle came back to my house. We sat outside and basked in the day, while we peppered each other with questions from the test. We got out an atlas to double-check our geography answers.

Back at college later that week, the class voted to accelerate our course schedule, attending classes every other night for four and a half hours so that we could finish sooner. Since I was a zombie, I did not vote for this speeded up finish. There was another reason, too, one that only a couple of us shared.

Michelle and I were misty-eyed to think that it would soon be over. She had been a sculptor and photographer before her career change. We had walked through the fire during our internships and risen from the ashes as new individuals. We had reinvented ourselves. We loved going to class. We would gladly have gone all summer. We could not imagine our future teaching careers without the support of the twelve people we had come to rely on as sounding boards, and for sustenance.

But the others were in a lather to get finished, and so we ended our campaign clocking fifteen class hours a week. The grand finale was a party at my house. Only seven people came. Some who had replied in the affirmative offered no explanation for not showing, save for one who called on a cell phone to say that she was furniture shopping on the North Side and caught in traffic. The dark sky poured rain all day long.

Chapter 46

Midnight Catches a Snake

On Sunday, Midnight caught a garden snake. I put it in a microwave container with a garden ecosystem, punched some holes for air and set it in the shade. Midnight later produced a second snake, so identical to the first that I had to look in the container to see if the other one was still there. It was. We released the second one, but I took the first to school on Monday.

Big hit! Everyone got to see it move around (quite gingerly, actually, considering it had a cat bite in its side) and flick its tongue. Martin, my naturalist, pleaded to take it home.

Second graders are natural scientists. They are fascinated with nature and driven to understand the physical world around them.

Earlier in the year we had studied wasps and ladybugs, because of the children's many questions about why these creatures were invading our human space. We had tons of yellow jackets on our playground every fall, swarming the school, flying in the windows and stinging scores of kids. Our research revealed that they were not bees but wasps. We learned: They are social insects, living together in communities; they don't sting if you don't bother them—they sting when they are "nervous"; they are "the paper-makers of the insect world"; they do not store food, so when fall comes, they act weird because they are hungry and getting ready to die.

We kept daily tallies of the number of wasps we observed. The number declined until the only wasps we saw were mostly in the garbage cans and only on warm, sunny mornings. We connected the weather forecast to their ultimate demise. One day we captured a wasp so large we concluded she must be the queen.

During a citywide ladybug infestation in October, we used information from the newspaper to learn why these biting orange bugs were different from their red relations, why they were introduced to the United States and how they migrated north to Chicago.

But the snake project was best of all. Everyone made snake books. They were divine. Some were accordion books made by folding a strip of paper like an accordion, some were pages stapled together. Some were scientific, some straightforward reporting about the presence of a snake in our room and its triumphant visit to the kindergarten room, borne by 401 students. Asophane did a research paper, adding complicated snake-related words of her own choosing from the dictionary. Mine was from the snake's point of view, describing the traumatic capture and jarring change of scene.

Spring break snuck up on us, and it was a blissful, endless series of chores in the garden. A startling amount of our backyard grass had died from neglect last year. I scattered bag after bag of seed. Growing grass, I quickly realized, was more trouble than having a newborn in the house. It had to be watered all the time. I wasn't changing diapers or nursing a baby, but I was grimy with dirt every day. Which was not cool because another neglected and long-put-off disaster, the bathroom, was being gutted and remodeled.

The first week back from break was paralyzing. I was too sapped to move. The children were unruly. I figured they spent as much time over vacation outside as I did. It was hard for all of us to be back indoors.

The outside temperature was eighty-five degrees, and our room, which had east-facing windows, was stifling by mid-morning. Only a few classrooms had working air conditioning. Mine was not one. We were sweaty and disagreeable. The fan put up a noble effort, but it was meager with all those sweaty little bodies sticking to their plastic chairs.

The listening lab broke, so I brought that table up front and proclaimed it the writer's workshop. Five students a day brought their journals. We sat in a circle and talked about our writing. It was hugely popular.

We had many thoughtful discussions about words and storytelling, about generating ideas and the imperative to write down the things that we wonder about, about how writing helps us figure things out.

My Iowa test prep materials, which I turned over for copying ten days earlier allotting time for practice, came to me half an hour after my class finished the Iowa test. It didn't matter, really. Testing second-graders was optional. I would never know how they did, but it was good practice for third grade, a "benchmark" year that mattered to the bean counters.

Chapter 47

Lost Parents

Asophane was not herself. She was cross and weepy, defiant and clingy. She stole boxes of cookies from our cupboard and stuffed them in her backpack. Her hair was a mess and her clothes were dirty. I sat with her on the stairwell outside our classroom and asked her what was going on.

"My mother is in jail," she said. Fat tears rolled down her face.

In the course of our year together, there had been hints that all was not well with Asophane's mother. One time, she slept all day when she should have been picking up her daughter's report card. When Asophane tried to wake her, she told the child to go pick it up herself. Asophane sneaked up to our classroom and made a case for picking up her own report card, but the rule was that they were to be handed over to parents only. I let Asophane see her report card and gave her cookies and juice. It was a good report card and she was dying to show it to her mother. It languished in the office until the next grading period.

The jail term was nearly as long as a grading period. Since Asophane was counting the days, I put her in charge of our classroom calendar. She was efficient. Every morning, she tacked the square for that day in its proper place. Every so often, she'd tell me how many more days it would be until her mother came home. A couple of times, she told me she would not be at school the next day, because she was going to visit her mother.

I'd been to Cook County Jail, and I imagined Asophane standing in line in that noisy, heartbreaking place, waiting her turn to talk to her mother in a small, airless room.

There was a big party at Asophane's grandmother's house when her mother was released. The months of worry had been hard on the child. She had been so self-assured, so fearless before. Happy as she was when it was over, she still seemed worried and subdued.

The same week Asophane's mother came home, the father of another second-grader got involved in a dispute with a couple of men two blocks from school. There was some sort of illicit activity involved, and whatever it was broke bad. He saw it coming and told his daughter to run.

Because the child ran, she was spared the sight of her father getting shot to death.

The school office had been notified by the police, and the child's teacher, a first-year intern, was informed first thing in the morning. Knowing her student, and how important her father had been in her life, the teacher was grief-stricken. She was surprised and unprepared when the child showed up for school that day and told her, "My daddy's dead."

The teacher put on a movie for the children and put her head down on her desk so the children wouldn't see her cry.

Chapter 48

Mother's Day

Mother's Day weekend found me in South Haven, Michigan, the place I go to reconnect with my truest self. I took Mia and a friend, but my real objective was to spend the short time away reflecting on my amazing two years that were nearly finished and look ahead to my future as a teacher.

It was very windy and cold but sunny. We walked the beach, went to town for a bit, then checked into a hotel. I thoroughly enjoyed the company of fifth graders They talk about the most amazing things. They wonder whether we are living in a parallel universe or whether we are really living on a crumb on a table of a much larger place without realizing our insignificance. They consider how weird it is that you can never really "see" your own face, only its reflection, and wonder whether what we see in the mirror is really what we look like to the rest of the world.

While the girls were shopping in town Saturday, I bought a *Kalamazoo Gazette*, the first paper I worked for right out of college. There was a front-page story about recruiting teachers from other professions. Michigan, like every other state in the nation, was facing a teacher shortage. Legislation to allow alternative certification had been written, but had no sponsor and therefore hadn't been introduced. The state was already feeling the teacher pinch as retirements soared. So I guessed I could move back to Michigan any time I wanted and have a job waiting. I'd also heard ads on the radio for a California teacher fair. The greatest needs in California were identical to Chicago's: teachers for special education, math, science and bilingual education.

On Sunday morning, Mother's Day, we revisited the beach. It was a splendid clear morning with the crisp spring air so unique to the Great

Lakes. The wind had died down, and the sun was warm. Not a cloud in the sky. One sailboat, one motorboat, seagulls. It was deserted, quiet, deliciously evocative. I settled myself in the sand and watched gentle waves lap the shore.

I thought about motherhood, the most consuming role of my life. I thought about how much mothering the second-graders needed and how poorly-equipped I often felt to do that job. I wondered whether my own two children needed that level of nurturing from their teachers.

I felt angry at parents who had let their children down, the parents who were in jail, on drugs, who were narcissistic at terrible expense to their kids. I was mad at the ones who beat and berate their children, who only gave attention when their children misbehaved and ignored them when they are jumping through hoops for positive attention. I was mad at the parents who abandoned their children, either physically or emotionally, leaving them adrift in the world, unable to make eye contact and refusing to speak. I was angry at the ones who ruined their lives with drugs to the point they couldn't provide a roof over their children's heads and the ones who stayed out all night and kept their kids up at all hours, in harm's way. I had two phone messages on the classroom phone the week before from a seven-year-old at a quarter to midnight. On the messages, she sang me songs about school and how she'd see me the next morning.

As a teacher, I could never fill those children's needs. That was what parents were for. What I could do seemed so small against the enormity of the risks some students faced, like a single wave nudging the shoreline of their lives. I was grateful for the parents and grandparents of my students who tended their children well. I was in awe of the single mothers who went back to school and of the parents who battled chronic illnesses and still put their children first.

I walked the beach and collected many beautiful stones of different colors, from ebony to alabaster, from teal to tangerine, rocks with pictures in them, rocks in the shapes of Africa, of hearts, rocks that were perfectly round or oblong, rocks with fossils, rocks with different textures, speckled stones, smooth stones. I would bring them to school the next day and tell the children I was thinking of them on Mother's Day and brought them treasures.

We would look at them dry and regard their shapes and textures. Then we would spray them with water and look at them wet, when their hidden personality and true, deep beauty is revealed.

They would choose whichever one they liked best. The one that represents their own self. They would write in their journals about their special rock and why they chose it.

I chose a picture rock. It looked like a yellow egg with a lacy black top and bottom, and seagulls flying in the middle.

After many false starts, we finally pried ourselves from the splendid beach and piled into the car for the drive back to Chicago. We listened to Terri Hemmert's "Rampant Beatlemania," a once-a-year radio extravaganza of ten straight hours of Beatles music on WXRT. I called twice to win trivia contests but couldn't get through. If I had, I would have asked Terri to dedicate "Yellow Submarine" to Room 401 from Mrs. B.

Back at school the next day, the children were thrilled by the Lake Michigan stones. They enjoyed looking at the myriad rocks in detail. Admittedly, the water sprayers got a little carried away, causing a minor flood, but it was so much fun to squeeze the spray bottle handles, who could blame them? The children looked and touched, picking up rocks, putting them back, studying another and another, agonizing over the one stone they loved the best. Ultimately, they made their choices.

"I pick this rock because it's my best color and it's colorful and pretty that's why I picked it and it's a heart," Natasha wrote.

"I like my rock because it is beautiful and soft and I like my rock because in the middle it is twirly and colorful and it look like a tornado," Tashequa wrote.

Hakim wrote a thank-you card: "Mrs. B, I love the rock! The rock is pretty! Thanks for the rock!" He drew a picture of his rock inside a heart.

When we hear the metaphor that someone's heart is like a stone, we think that they are so hardened they cannot love. In second grade, we managed to turn stone into tangible evidence of love and that is what I remember.

Chapter 49

Guns of Summer

As the days grew hotter and the leaves on the trees spread out new and green, a kid threatened to "go home and get my mama's gun and come back up here and shoot" his sixth-grade teacher, a first-year intern. The teacher called the cops. The police searched the boy's locker. The teacher, a cop and the boy went to the office, where the child continued to make shooting gestures (index finger pointed, thumb up, whispering "pow, pow, pow") at the teacher behind the policeman's back. The cop saw him and the police took the kid away. The child was soon back but not the teacher.

I happened to be punching in the following Monday morning, when the wife of the teacher who was threatened called him in sick. Whether out of fear or out of insult, he never came back. With ten days to go in the school year, another ship-jumper was unable to endure another minute. A year's worth of work down the drain seemed a better deal. I never heard of him again.

What would I have done, I wondered? How could an adult go back into that classroom and face that child again, knowing that every day would be a showdown, never knowing what might happen? At our school, such incidents were minimized as empty threats or, as the kids said time and again, "just playing with you." How were we supposed to decide when someone was not playing? As we lay bleeding? Yet at school, that teacher's defection was viewed as an overreaction. He was thought to be a silly white man, frightened off by a kid. He was a quitter, a failure. He didn't have what it took.

I wanted to call in sick. My kids had been horrible. I gave detention to six of them, which was twenty-four percent of the class. All but about a half-dozen others deserved it. With the hot weather, the whole place was up for grabs once again. Children were running amok, and the teachers were outnumbered, beaten down, powerless to stop them, it seemed. If only we could hold on until the last bell.

I was so overwhelmed that I barely noticed until Louis collapsed that he had read eighteen pages of *Go Dog Go!* He was so exhausted that he staggered from the stairwell into the room and immediately put his head down on the desk. When I patted his back as I walked by, he was sweaty. That meant it really did happen. Louis read a book. I experienced a blip of joy.

As the grisly end wore down, I did what I had done the year before: I let go of the non-behavers and showered my time and attention on the ones who were still working. They bloomed like flowers. I savored our time together in the way that people do when the hourglass is running out.

I did a mental count of the teacher interns who had come through the doors and who had left. By my tally, sixteen interns came on board in my two years. All but five left in one circumstance or another.

Of the original seven, only Astrid and I survived.

The next year, we started with Astrid, me, a first-grade replacement and four fresh interns. Of the four new interns, three left: that first-grade teacher with the frightened eyes, the second-grade teacher who used to sell insurance and the one who was threatened with shooting.

At his behest, Astrid tried to get the "quitter's" things out of his locked classroom, using the ruse that he had things belonging to her that she needed. The principal told her in clipped tones, "Since you're his messenger, tell him he needs to go through the principal."

In an incredible display of self-restraint, Astrid kept her mouth shut and left the office. But she sat quaking with rage in her car for a long time afterward, contemplating whether to go back in and tell the principal to shove it up his ass. I wonder what he would have done if she'd gone back in and told him she was going to go home and get her mama's gun and come back and shoot him.

Chapter 50

Going from Here

I was talking to my mom a couple of days later, and she asked what I had lined up for fall.

"Nothing," I said. "But the phone will ring."

I had made only one effort to find another job. I had written to the principal who had come up to me after a speech I gave to the Annenberg Foundation a year before, a woman with a short blond Afro and fantastic jewelry who told me, "When you're done with your internship, call me. I like your attitude."

When I told people I wanted to teach at her school, they laughed and said, "Right, everyone wants to teach there." The school was known throughout the city as an exciting school that works for kids. They said it in such a way that implied I didn't have a prayer of ever teaching there.

The day after I talked to my mother, that principal called me to set up an interview. When I returned her call at 5:40 p.m., she answered the office phone herself. I was not surprised. By then, I understood the extraordinary dedication it took to be a strong school leader.

"Are you going to wax the floors on your way out of the building?" I asked her.

"No," she cracked, "I already did that."

We had a conversation about the importance of recess, the topic of my master's inquiry project, and how her school had a 3:15 dismissal so the kids get recess at lunchtime and the teachers get a forty-five-minute breather to set up the afternoon.

I set my sights on this school and this leader. I did not make any other calls, though I checked out the Chicago Public Schools job listings web site. There were tons of openings, especially in the upper grades. I also stopped in the office at my children's school near home to sniff around one afternoon, but the principal had left.

I turned down an offer to teach graduate journalism students over the summer at Northwestern University, because an undergraduate algebra class at one of the City Colleges, necessary to fulfill a teacher certification requirement, would require my complete attention. I felt ill-equipped to teach a bunch of motivated rich kids anyway. I was so far removed from where they wanted to go, it wouldn't be fair.

The end of the school year trudged on at a tormentingly slow pace. Though I hadn't been eaten alive, as one veteran educator had predicted, I felt bitten and torn about my extremities. My mood was dour. I snapped at my students all week, then kicked my children's friends out of my house at 10:30 Friday night, after more than fourteen hours with the shrill voices of children ringing in my ears that day. "Go home," I told them, the first time I'd ever asked someone to leave my home. I just couldn't take any more. I was an open wound. Over the three-day Memorial Day weekend, I slept ten hours one night, eight the next and eleven hours Sunday night. I woke up feeling nearly human, and I thought I recognized a glimmer of the person who used to be me before she got so cranky and ornery and snappish. That night, I watched Ken Burns' *Jazz* documentary. One of Count Basie's band members said he slept for a year after leaving his orchestra. I know exactly how he felt. I could have spent months curled in bed.

With bags under my eyes, wearing a ridiculous flowered dress and a jean jacket, I went for my interview at the new school. The day happened to be the day of the annual school carnival.

I arrived as students were being dismissed. I announced myself and settled on the office bench. Directly in my sightline was a small quilt, hanging from a nail on the office counter. "All you need is love," it said in red blocky letters, amid floating red hearts.

The principal asked me to walk with her to a back door that opened onto a playground where cleanup was in progress. In the office, I had already seen digital images of the day's action. The big hit of the day was a giant slide that was an inflatable model of the *Titanic*, in sinking position, which people climbed up and slid down. There had been food, games, tattoos, face painting, a petting zoo and pony rides. Some kids were still trying to finish enormous dill pickles on sticks. Seagulls wheeled and cried over the blacktop, looking for scraps to scavenge. We were a mile nearer the lake than my neighborhood. There would always be seagulls here.

I couldn't believe how many children's names the principal knew. As the students left the building, they were walking, not running. They kept their hands to themselves. They did not touch one another. Most were quiet, but if they were talking, it was in normal conversational tones, not screaming. At least twenty kids said to their principal as they left, "Thanks for the carnival." It was jarring to hear children saying thank you.

We talked for nearly two hours. About teaching children. About testing. About assessment. About curriculum integration. About teams of teachers working collaboratively. The school, with corridors that looked like a museum of African art, had three bands, sports teams, after-school dance and art programs, an entrepreneurship initiative and video club and book clubs, among other programs. We talked about a school paper and what she and the vice principal would like to see on a fifth-grade reading list.

I showed my portfolio and described some of the cross-curricular projects my classes had done in seventh and second grades. She liked the growth charts we kept with our spring planting project. The vice principal liked the dream trip. They both liked the naming ceremony. The vice principal wanted to know how I liked second grade. It was a loaded question. I said I was glad for the experience but would not care to repeat it. I said I couldn't handle the neediness of the students, it was just too grueling. I patted her on the arm and said her name ten times in a row. We laughed. I said I wouldn't mind working my way up to seventh or eighth grade again someday, but the fifth-grade opening they had sounded just right to me as my youngest daughter had just finished fifth, and I knew it well.

I asked point-blank how they felt about a teacher who was also a writer and whether they thought the outside world needed to know what was really going on in schools today. Could they bear to have a colleague who told the stories? I promised that I would do my best to walk the line, to be honest without violating anyone's privacy, exploiting children or harming the innocent. I assured them that I was a teacher first now, but I would always be a storyteller.

I realized that I was poised on the brink of an excellent opportunity to see in action the kind of leadership that made this school stand out among 700 elementary schools in our city. I very much wanted to be part of an organization working hard, plowing forward. The faculty was dedicated, innovative, bright. Initiative was applauded. Everyone wore many hats. There were responsibilities to serve on committees, to formulate policies and philosophies. It was a unique team, constantly evolving, positive.

"I'm going to do something strange and forgo the secret conference with the vice principal and listen to my heart," the principal said. "I'm going to offer you the job right now."

I accepted, on the spot, with sincere gratitude and humility. I thought, "I will do anything for this woman." I got up and hugged her.

"We'll be here all summer," she said.

"So will I," I said. "So will I."

Chapter 51

Graduation

When I had playground duty on Monday mornings, I liked to stand in the corner of the playground near the busiest intersection. From there I felt like I saw the big picture.

I could see kids coming and going from the store across the street, eating chips and drinking soda pop for breakfast. I saw children arrive at school at a run, slipping inside the fence with joy and exuberance at seeing their schoolmates. I loved the deep, pounding beat of the bouncing basketballs under the high slap of the jump ropes and the chorus of voices filling out the middle.

I saw the long picture. I saw children who had been abandoned in heartless ways early in their lives making their way in the world. I saw children who needed our school because it was the only consistent thing in their lives. I saw children who had endured incalculable losses who were still able to learn and to love. Some I knew well enough to see their dreams and aspirations taking shape.

I asked my mentor if she could watch my class so I could go to graduation and see my former seventh-grade students walk across the stage.

"I always work graduation," she said, "so I can't do it. I line up the students. But I'll see what I can do to get someone to take your class."

I suppose many teachers who had been at a school a long time would see all the graduates as their former students. But there's something about a teacher's first class that is like a parent's firstborn. I really wanted to go, but experience had left me with little hope that someone would show up to relieve me on my outpost come graduation day. I tried to cobble together my own plan. It didn't help that no one could give me a straight answer on the actual day of graduation or the time.

On what turned out to be graduation day, my second graders happened to have library at 9:40. I'd gotten wind that graduation was occurring about that time. I dropped them off, grabbed my umbrella and dashed through the freezing rain to the other building, dripping past my old classroom on my way down the hallway to the auditorium.

"Hi, Mrs. B.," said Pierre, who was standing in the hallway outside the auditorium. I gave him a hug. He looked well. He said he was doing all right. He said he had graduated the day before. I gave him my hearty congratulations.

"You know how he lies," the security guard said as I opened the door and walked through.

The auditorium was full. I walked to the back, where I could see everything and everyone.

I saw Eric and Andre and Racquel walk down the aisle. I saw Kyisha on stage and Nichelle, Cortez, DeVille and everyone else. They were in bright gold gowns, singing "Hallelujah in the Tabernacle." Donna had once again channeled the students' talents into a stage spectacular. She smiled and waved at me from the front and left, next to the turd section.

The children's voices soared above the drone of talking from the audience. I waved to parents I knew and they smiled and waved back to me, joyful and proud, cameras in hand. Some of my second graders were there for siblings or cousins. The valedictorian was one of the three girls I had taken to the Sunday open-house at the all-girls school in the dead of winter sixth months before. Many others had speaking parts, and I was so proud of every one of them my face hurt from smiling. They seemed much more polished than last year.

My mentor scurried past. "I see you made it after all," she observed.

At 10:19 I tore myself away and picked up my second graders.

That afternoon, I went to an awards ceremony of The Rochelle Lee Fund, which provides classroom books to about 400 Chicago teachers every year if they write a proposal and attend four days' worth of workshops to learn the best ways to teach reading. It was the second year I'd won the award, and it was a godsend. My school did not allow children to check books out of the library, but children in 401 were required to take books, really good books, home from the classroom library daily as their reading homework. *Chicago Tribune* columnist Mary Schmich, my former competition, was our speaker. She told a great story about her mother hiding in the bathroom to read.

Later that week, the second graders and I finished *Charlotte's Web*, my favorite book. Asophane read the last part for me, because I always cry at the end. It's the second-to-last paragraph that gets me every time: "It was the best place to be, thought Wilbur, this warm delicious cellar, with the garrulous geese, the changing seasons, the heat of the sun, the passage of swallows, the nearness of rats, the sameness of sheep, the love of spiders, the smell of manure and the glory of everything." To revel in one's place in the world, barn or classroom, fast lane or busted-up sidewalk, is a rare gift. The children jumped out of their seats to see whether my tears were real.

"It's okay," I explained. "If a book makes you cry, that means it is a really good book. It made you feel something you really believe in your heart."

On Thursday, Paul Vallas resigned as the chief executive officer of the Chicago Public Schools after six years. A new era lay ahead.

That afternoon, before our staff development meeting, the principal handed out the assignment list for next year. I was listed for second grade. I had filled out a preference sheet listing fifth grade as my first choice, then fourth grade and finally seventh grade. Astrid's name was not on the sheet. I looked at her with my eyebrows raised and saw she was crying. She explained later that she had asked several times for a preference sheet, which no one ever supplied for her. Suspicious, she asked her mentor what was going on and was told to talk to the principal. She was very upset and rightfully. It was underhanded, exclusionary and mean. She was a sensitive person, so it was also cruel. She would find another job without any trouble. But not being asked to stay was hurtful.

The principal informed the staff that our school was among the 200 lowest-performing schools in the city and would begin a new reading program, with scripted lessons the following year. That would be the imposed curriculum for ninety minutes a day. We were given the summer school list, which made no sense at all. Some of my better readers were on it, kids who could even read cursive. I could not explain this development to their parents. I told Hakim's mother that the decision was based on one test in which the children read aloud to a stranger.

"If he goes, it won't hurt him. It'll sharpen his skills. You are a good mother. You know what he needs. If you think the test is bogus, talk to the office and have him retake it," I advised her. He had taken books home every day.

I hadn't told anyone I was leaving. My standard answer to the gossips was, "I have not spoken to the principal yet." I doled out my prized possessions, some of which were not even mine, to other teachers. The second-grade teacher who was so helpful to me got the globe I had liberated from the library, dusty with neglect, months earlier, and a set of lovely science books. The kindergarten teacher got the tiny little table and chairs that served as our writers' workshop.

As the week and the school year bumped to a close, fewer students attended school regularly. Our room was quite empty.

On the last day, I handed my principal my resignation letter, informing him that I had accepted another teaching position in the Chicago Public Schools.

"Teaching both seventh grade and second grade here gave me a broad perspective and rich experience. Thank you."

The principal read the letter out loud. He smiled.

"I know you will be successful," he said.

"Thank you," I said, reaching out to shake his hand.

That was it. No "Wish you were staying," no "What can we do to keep you?" No mention of "remediation."

Brandon and Tashequa and their older siblings helped me load up my last things, the baskets of books from our classroom library. Those books were like old familiar friends to us, their spines taped and covers curled from the wear of small hands turning their pages day after day for nearly forty weeks.

Before we left, we looked around the peach-colored classroom. We decided to leave intact our *Charlotte's Web* bulletin board and our sentence strips above the board about who we are. Standing in the doorway, we read them all again, out loud, taking turns:

"We read a lot of books."

"We write in our journals."

"Our favorite food is pizza."

"We are learning ballet."

"We are getting our grown-up teeth."

"We keep lists."

"We have snack time."

"We know all about wasps."

"We had a snake."

"We love the Beatles."

"We work in the doctor's office."

"We sing every day."

We wanted the class coming after us to know who had been there before, who we were. We walked out together, making a racket. We passed through the brown metal doors and went down the concrete steps. On the other side of the fence, Louis was hanging by his knees from the monkey bars. He waved to us, upside down. His bookbag was on the ground nearby.

"Don't forget your bookbag, Louis," I called, pointing to where it lay.

He grinned in response, dangling, his arms outstretched.

"Cree! Cree!" the seagulls protested, rising and scattering as our jabbering group crossed the parking lot.

Postscript

In November 2001 Donnamaria Gamble married Charles Baker in a joyous celebration at St. Sabina Church in Chicago. True to form, the bride staged a spectacular melding of African tradition with her boundless love of the Lord. There were dancers and drummers and a wedding party of twelve. The rafters rang.

Two months later, many of the same people gathered in the same church for Donna's funeral after she died suddenly of a heart attack at age forty-eight.

Many of our former students were present at the service. Through them, my departed friend, who had already given me so much, gave me one last gift: the realization that the connections between all of us would endure.

These did not end after one year or two or even after a lifetime. We were woven into each other's lives and memories for all time. We would cross paths in the unknown future as certainly as destiny had reconnected us that sad night. The influence of teachers on the lives of children, and of children on their teachers, goes on and on.

Index